PRAISE FOR
BACK TO WORK AFTER BABY

"Lori Mihalich-Levin's new book is a gem. Filled with engaging stories and imminently practical advice, Mihalich-Levin not only tackles the complicated logistics of planning for a leave and return, but gets to the heart of the matter: the stories we tell ourselves. Women's lives have changed utterly, yet cultural expectations have yet to catch up. Mihalich-Levin shows new mothers how to clear a path through the noise and find their own way. Reading the book is like having coffee with a wise friend who assures you, "You've got this."

— Brigid Schulte | Award-winning journalist and author of *The New York Times* bestselling *Overwhelmed: Work, Love & Play When No One has the Time* and director of The Better Life Lab at New America

"This book is what every new mother needs, but just doesn't know it. It is a must-read for practical reasons, with invaluable coping tips, and for emotional reasons, reminding us women that we are not alone. There is a sisterhood out there, and Lori's book gives permission and a path to tap into it. Bravo!"

— Dana Bash | Chief Political Correspondent, CNN

"It's all here! In Back to Work After Baby: How to Plan and Navigate a Mindful Return from Maternity Leave, *Lori Mihalich-Levin pulls together everything you need to navigate the tricky territory of motherhood in today's workplace. This guide is both intensely personal and very practical, crammed with real-world advice from negotiating your time off to pumping at work. My favorite section deals with making your return work for you, leveraging your maternal interlude so that you come back more confident, capable, and calm than when you left. No matter where you work or what you do, this book is for you."*

— Valerie Young | Public Policy Analyst, Mom-mentum

BACK TO WORK AFTER BABY

How to Plan and Navigate
a Mindful Return from
Maternity Leave

Lori Mihalich-Levin, JD

A portion of the proceeds from the sale of this book will benefit the First Shift Justice Project and its mission to empower low-income pregnant women and parents to safeguard the health and economic security of their families by asserting their workplace rights.
www.firstshift.org

Back to Work After Baby:
How to Navigate a Mindful Return from Maternity Leave

Mihalich-Levin, Lori, author.
    Back to work after baby : how to plan and navigate a
    mindful return from maternity leave / by Lori
    Mihalich-Levin.
        pages cm
        Includes bibliographical references.
        ISBN 978-0-692-82163-3

        1. Working mothers. 2. Working mothers--Psychology.
        3. Maternity leave. 4. Women--Employment re-entry.
        5. Working mothers--Social networks. 6. Work-life balance.
        I. Title.

        HQ759.48.M54 2017   306.874'3
                           QBI17-900006

Copy Editing + Cover & Interior Design
Melissa Tenpas —www.MelissaTenpas.com
Cover Photograph | iStockPhoto

CONTENTS

This book is dedicated to:

ALL mamas who are currently pregnant, on maternity leave right now, and who have already returned to work. You are strong. Brilliant. Amazing. And enough.

To everyone who has mothered *me* along the way, throughout life.

And above all, to Team Red.

Chapter 1

INTRODUCTION

Welcome, readers. Welcome to this journey called motherhood. Called "working mother." Called "balance" or "juggling" or "having it all." Or, just simply, called life.

I am delighted you have joined me in these pages to explore the new world you are creating and navigating. I hope that by reading about these experiences—both my own and those of awesome working mothers who have generously shared here—you will feel the sense of "me too" that I have come to find so powerful.

This is my story, yes, and a map of my own path through some of the early challenges of life with baby. But it is also the story of so, so many other moms who have come before me. Take comfort in knowing that you are not alone in any of this, mama. Yes, your feelings are strong and personal. And, they are not unique. Take comfort in the community of amazing mothers whose ranks you are now joining and who, if you let them, will guide you skillfully into this next phase of your life.

WHY I CREATED MINDFUL RETURN

I am a planner by nature. When I was pregnant, WOW did I nest. I had name lists ready to go the day we learned the baby's sex. My husband and I visited one day care per month during my pregnancy. I took a weekly prenatal yoga class and soaked in a few pages of Karen Mazen Miller's *Momma Zen* each night before bed. I ordered and set up the crib before I got too big. I read Harvey Karp's *Happiest Baby on the Block* on the beach on our "babymoon." I also did the requisite nesting cleaning, somehow managing to find and remove dirt from every slat in our bathroom window blinds. Pregnancy does strange things to the mind.

So it was only natural I would give some thought to my maternity leave and my ultimate return to the office. During my first pregnancy, I had a vague notion of how long I wanted to be out, a boss who was flexible about my return, and a few thoughts about not wanting to check my work email until I came back.

I really didn't think much about going back to work, though—how my return would go, how I wanted it to look and feel, or how I could plan a meaningful return. I did some web searching for advice on returning to work after a maternity leave, and I did not turn up much that I found helpful.

There were endless lists on the internet, of course—"Five Top Tips" here, "10 Survival Strategies" there—but nothing that actually helped me plan a mindful return. Was there some helpful practical advice out there, like "bring extra breast pads to work because you might leak"? Yes. Were there funny stories about new mothers' inabilities to carry on adult conversation? Yes. Was there snarky advice I couldn't relate to, like "don't show your baby pictures to anyone lest they never take you seriously in your career"? Absolutely. But, nothing that truly spoke to me.

I concluded from this dearth of intel on what it's *really* like to go back to work, and on how to make it go more smoothly, that (a) this must be something people don't think too much about; (b) it cannot possibly be all that bad; and (c) I will just figure something out. And for the most part, I muddled through. My first return to work had its challenges, but overall it went relatively smoothly. Enter a second child, and I was in for a shock.

Perhaps it was that by Baby Number Two, I had a more demanding job, or perhaps it was trying to juggle a toddler and a baby on even less sleep than before. Perhaps it was a lot of internal pressure and unrealistic expectations. Perhaps it was feeling isolated and not talking to other moms who were going through the same thing at the same time. For whatever reason, my second return to work was a low point for me emotionally; full of more nights than I care to admit when I found myself crying as I sat on the kitchen floor.

Since my second return from maternity leave in the summer of 2013, I have thought a lot about how to make the experience of heading back to work less stressful. Less anxiety-ridden. Less exhausting. Motivated to take action and improve the state of return-to-work for other mamas, I started a community at my office where I have heard the stories and picked the brains of women who—like me—had gone through the same transitions.

Next, I created a blog called Mindful Return (MindfulReturn.com/blog), dedicated to offering information and advice to women planning their return to work. Then, I developed the online Mindful Return Course (MindfulReturn.com/e-course), which teaches working mothers new skills around healthy mindsets, logistics, leadership, and the importance of staying in community. It has brought together hundreds of mamas in a secure, online platform, who are all going through the same struggles at the same time. Now, I am sharing these journeys with you through this book, in the hopes you will feel more empowered and less alone.

Returning from maternity leave should not be something you have to "get through," but rather something you get to create. You will return to work a different person than when you left, with new skills that are—yes, indeed—useful at the office. You will have different priorities and goals, and you will likely be sleep deprived those first few months just trying to figure things out. This is a new, exciting phase of life, and it is worth being thoughtful and intentional . . . not terrified.

Let's explore here, together, how to plan, create, and navigate a mindful return.

RETURNING IS A 3-D PUZZLE

Returning to work from maternity leave is not a one-dimensional issue. If you ask the average person what a new mom has to grapple with upon her return, the first thing that will probably come to mind is probably pumping at work or child care. Returning to work after maternity leave is not just about pumping or about all those logistics and details that need to be figured out to make it work.

Yes, of course, to have a successful return to work, a new mother needs to figure out how to nourish her baby, how to find a child care provider she trusts, and how to get out the door (relatively) on time and without spit-up all over herself in the morning. And you *will* get helpful tips on all these logistical issues (Chapter 3).

But to have a calm, mindful, and well-planned return, a new mother needs to think about much more. So many aspects of her identity, physical and mental health, work skills and strengths, and support network are suddenly on the table, and it is worth spending time thinking about these other elements of returning, too. That's why this book also focuses on a new mama's mindset (Chapter 2), her ability to use her leave as a leadership opportunity (Chapter 4), and the importance of staying connected to a supportive community (Chapter 5).

When I was returning to work after maternity leave, I certainly did not view my return in the three-dimensional way I am advocating here (though I wish I had). I spent entirely too much energy—particularly during and after my first leave—worrying about how I would get "caught up" on the work I missed, the idea that my value to my employer was somehow declining as I left work at 4:30 pm each day and took time out to pump, and of course how my baby could possibly be faring okay in my absence. I did not connect much with other moms who were going through the same thing. And I certainly did not view it as important to carve out time for myself. As you might guess, this wasn't exactly an empowering way to think about my return, and it certainly wasn't a recipe for good physical or mental health.

If you are returning to work and want not only to "get through" this period of time but to live it fully, love it deeply, and radiate as the brilliant mama and professional you are, I encourage you to look through all these different lenses at the whole return rather than just one piece of it.

By focusing on your mindset, logistics, leadership, and community, I guarantee you will feel more prepared for your return. You will also keep in perspective those many dimensions of the beautiful mama you are and keep you focused on savoring that miracle of a being you have created.

WHY THE "MINDFUL" IN MINDFUL RETURN

When I set out to find a way to help mamas in this period of transition, growing into a new life with baby while also returning to work, I debated what to call this project. What was I hoping new mamas would learn? How to have a "successful return"? A "peaceful return"? An "authentic return"? Build a community of women all going through this at the same time? Yes, yes, yes, and yes. But the path to all of these, I believe, is to return to work mindfully.

If you consult Wikipedia, you will see mindfulness defined as "the intentional, accepting and non-judgmental focus of one's attention on the emotions, thoughts and sensations *occurring in the present moment*." I have also seen it defined as recognizing the small acts of our daily lives, and paying attention to our thoughts and feelings without judging them. **All of which I'll sum up as simply: Be present. Be here. Be here NOW.**

Being mindful in this space of returning to work has two steps, I think. The first is **thoughtfully planning the heck out of a number of baby- and work-related things,** so you can bring more of your attention away from the future and into the present. For me, this involved everything from lists on the fridge of meals for everyone for the next day, to carefully researching and selecting a day care provider, to intentionally finding communities of new moms, to writing out a morning brain-dump task list at work, so I could get the swirling to-dos out of my head and onto paper.

Then, the second step is **actually being here now.** I am not talking about spending your days meditating—though I do believe meditation is a useful tool (and spending a few days in silence sounds like a heavenly experience!)—but I am talking about being present. REALLY witnessing how your baby's soft, fine, hair feels when you run your hand over it; REALLY watching your partner learn how to make your baby giggle; REALLY being present for your direct report who is talking through a work challenge in your office; REALLY exploring new ways to do research or lead a team.

Personally, I get to the second step more easily, if I have done the first. If I know dinner is planned and bottles are made, I can delight in those pre-meal squeals of laughter and watch my baby's surprise as he bumps up and down in the red wagon I'm pulling over some rocks in our back yard. If I know what's on tap for my week at work (okay, at least in theory, if my kids aren't sick . . . . . .), I can truly be present in the meetings I attend and can focus on why I'm sitting there.

So let's think here about returning to work mindfully. With a little help, *I know* that you can and will tackle all the logistics of returning to work, so you can feel confident, knowledgeable, peaceful, and ready to be present to the magnificent family, career, and life you are creating.

Chapter 2

A MINDFUL MINDSET FOR RETURN

If you are anything like I was, you try not to think too much about the end of your maternity leave. At all. (Or if you're already back at work, you tried to avoid the subject as long as possible while you were out!) But, if you are anything like me, you secretly wished you could think about your return in a peaceful, somewhat less terrified, healthy way—one that let you do the planning and growing you needed to, but without all the fear and without all the worry.

"I don't want to think about something terrifying like returning. I want to spend all my mental energy on my amazing new baby," I thought. (And the funny thing is, I really did like my job.) "I'll think about it later," I promised myself.

When thoughts about the end of my maternity leave inevitably crept in, though, all I could think was "Agh! I don't know how that's going to work." "I'm going to be a mess." "Oh, to have a nice, quiet office with only adults around and no barf would be AWESOME right now . . . " "How can I possibly leave my baby?" And of course crazy things like "Oh [bleep]. Baby is refusing to take a bottle. If I took him to day care he'd die, so I'm never going to be able to leave his side and will never be able to go back to work!" The catastrophizing can get funny.

As I read on an awesome blog called Tiny Buddha (TinyBuddha.com), though, *"a moment can't possibly radiate fully when you're suffocating it in fear."*

You want this pregnancy, this time with your baby, these first few weeks back at work, and your love for your new baby to *radiate*, mama. You want to let your new life as a new family radiate. You want the new you in your career to radiate.

This chapter is all about reducing those fears by doing some important work on building confidence, practicing gratitude, gaining perspective, combating being overwhelmed, allowing yourself your feelings, managing new mama anxiety, and committing to self-care.

MINDFUL MINDSET: BUILDING CONFIDENCE

The mere fact that you are reading this book is brave. You have dared to think about returning rather than avoiding the subject of returning to work, and you are taking steps to learn how to make it a positive experience for you. As you read these chapters, I hope you will see yourself learning new things, getting calmer about the whole experience, and being able to think about return as an opportunity for you, your family, and your career to be in a healthy place. You will be growing muscles that will get stronger and stronger over time. As they do, I hope you will be more confident that you *can* be the author of the kind of return you want to have.

You probably have never had a baby before and figured out how to fit these pieces of life together. Or if you have done it before, perhaps you have never done it with two (or more!) little ones in tow. Take a deep breath, and realize that there is no way you *could* possibly know how this will all work, having not been through it before. Let yourself off the hook for being anxious, worried, or afraid. We all are.

Know, however, that you *have* done new things before. You have tackled new challenges and overcome big obstacles. You got through patches in life you thought would crush you. Can you think of a time when something else in your life was new and scary? Can you remember how you used your resources to figure out what to do next? How you put one foot in front of the other? Can you remember what it felt like to come out confident on the other side?

You've got this, mama. You've got this baby thing. You've got this work thing. You've got this doing both thing. You may not know it yet, but you really do.

MINDFUL MINDSET: PRACTICING GRATITUDE

A few months into my own return to work after my second child, I had hit rock bottom. I was a puddle of tears on the kitchen floor each evening and was letting a sense of being overwhelmed eat me alive. Or so it felt.

I had the good fortune at that critical moment to discover Shawn Fink's blog (then called *Awesomely Awake*, and now called *The Abundant Mama* at AbundantMama.com), and I signed up for her Abundant Mama Project online course (AbundantMama.com/abundant-mama-project). Through the four-week course, she inspired me to start a gratitude practice—one that truly saved my sanity. Because of her, I now remember, daily, to be grateful for my babes' soft skin. That even if there is food *under* the table, there is also food *on* it. And that I had a career to return to.

I have invited Shawn, founder of The Abundant Mama Project, to share with us here her own story of returning to work after maternity leave and her views on the importance of gratitude.

HERE ARE SHAWN FINK'S THOUGHTS ON THE IMPORTANCE OF GRATITUDE

I still remember my first lunch hour as a newly back-to-work mom.

Granted, I had been home for nearly two years with my twin daughters, but as I walked around town, amongst a sea of strangers, I felt like I was in some sort of twilight zone, and I was the zombie. The new mom zombie.

As the mom of two 2-year-olds, I was still exhausted. My clothes weren't ideal. Life was crazy, and I was adding a demanding, 9 to 5 job on top of it all.

And then there was that feeling . . . . . . the loss. The empty feeling of my babies not being with me.

There were some tears in that first week. Many tears.

But, through it all, I found my grounding and stayed strong, and I know my gratitude practice helped me through it.

The important thread through all of my mother-hood years has been my Abundant Mama gratitude practice. I say thanks all day long. I say it, write it, think it, and declare it.

It all began as a working mom when I found myself feeling tired, burned out and resentful—or, what I call the Land of Bitter and Sour.

The second I "experimented" with a gratitude practice, I was hooked. Good feelings washed over me. I had so much in my life as a mom.

Time with our children is limited when we work. We feel guilt for those lost days, those lost hours. We feel guilty for enjoying a quiet, peaceful lunch with no one crying or whining in our ears.

It isn't always easy. Mornings are tough. Our bosses and co-workers leave us feeling frustrated. And we're tired. So. Very. Tired.

When you find yourself headed toward the Land of Bitter and Sour, I suggest you to start saying this mantra: **Find the Good.**

I invite you to take the time to stop and "Find the Good" at least once in your day, or snap a photo, if you wish. There's even an app called Gratitude 365 for you to use on the go, when feeding in the chair, when walking out the door of day care. Here's how it works. You find some reason to go outside of your office— even if it's the bathroom—and stop and say, Find the Good.

And then find it.

Here are some ways to give yourself time to relish what's good in your life. You can take those moments anytime, but I love including these moments in my workday:

- Step outside and look up at the sky.
- Find a special quiet place and just sit, eyes closed.
- Hug your child in the morning.
- Write in your journal over lunch break.
- Eat a piece of chocolate from your desk drawer.
- Brew a cup of coffee or tea and feel the warmth in your hands.
- Stare out the window or at a special photo.
- Read a framed quote or a passage you love.
- Splash warm water on your face or apply lotion to your hands.

Returning to work is a bittersweet feeling. It's a major life change. And it's stressful and heartbreaking. But when you can track the abundance you already have in your life, that's where the light lives in your spirit. Start the practice now and keep it going, especially on the weekends and crazy Monday mornings.

Can you pause for a moment, right now, mama, and "find the good." What do you see?

MINDFUL MINDSET: GAINING PERSPECTIVE

Introducing that new and amazing human being into your world changes you. It changes the family system you live in and changes the professional system you work in. You *will* have a new vantage point on life than you did before you got pregnant—one you can use to see things in ways you never could.

To help us look through the perspective of women who are experienced mothers, supervisors, and leaders, I want to introduce you to the wisdom of two fantastic women:

- Dr. Coleen Kivlahan, one of my own mentors and teachers. Coleen was my boss during my second pregnancy and maternity leave, and she *got my experience* deep down. Whether exhausted and sleep deprived, or glowing and giddy, she understood what I was going through and was always there to offer advice, the longer view, and pure empathy.

- Tracy Fink, the Director of the Executive Women's Forum at CohnReznick, LLP. Tracy is now an empty nester, and she shares with us some fantastic advice for new mamas from "the other side." (In short, we can all calm down, breathe, and enjoy the ride a bit more!)

You will note some similarities between their advice. We need stories like Coleen's and Tracy's to remind us to zoom out and *trust* that our best is indeed good enough.

HERE ARE COLEEN KIVLAHAN'S THOUGHTS ON BEING PRESENT AS A MOTHER AND A PROFESSIONAL

It was 1979 (really?!!), when I came back to work as a resident doctor after my first baby was born. I had worked throughout my pregnancy, and up to one hour before labor began in earnest. Imagine being a young passionate, focused professional (yes, you . . .), then discovering that you love being home with your new baby, then wondering WHY you would ever want to go back to work?

Well, I too, wondered about my sanity, my emotional health, my professional future during that time. The thought of going back to work and dropping off my new baby with a stranger was frightening. The thought of not being the best doctor I could be, and being diverted by parenting, was foreign.

There is a very private story I can share with you that changed my perspective forever. One evening after work, my son and I were at a swimming lesson in a large pool. I had finished a very busy day at work, my mind was still on my day, and on tomorrow. I was in the pool with many other mothers and new babies. My son was reveling in the water and splashing with his hands on the surface of the water. Suddenly I saw a little brown blob float right by me. I thought

"This came from some other baby!" But NO . . . in my hurry mode, I had neglected to adequately secure the diaper and swim trunks and they leaked. From MY baby. The entire pool was then cleared for this public health emergency.

That night, my son looked up at me with such joy, he touched my heart in a whole new way, and suddenly I developed PERSPECTIVE.

I started laughing and could not stop. I fell in love. Truly, madly, deeply. And realized I had just had a moment of such grace and clarity, I would never be the same. I could deeply engage in being a mother AND a doctor.

I knew this was my work as a woman, a parent and a professional: to learn how to be fully present in each part of my life. To recognize that joy and peace come from seeing the things that are right in front of me and being grateful. Every day.

Reentry strategies that work:

Plan ahead (child care packing; work packing; car packing; meal planning); get up earlier to have some time alone every day; keep exercising; consider working 75-80% time if possible (just a few hours a week make a difference); connect with other moms for support; have a conversation with your boss about her or his expectations (transparency matters); share the duties with your family/partner/spouse or friends who can help; and set specific goals at work that you are likely to actually achieve (so you can feel good about something in your day!).

What is much harder to prepare for are the "new world" experiences:

The sudden onset of an extreme guilt attack (could be about work, your baby, or both); days when you call the day care more than five times just to check in; mornings when you wake up to fevers, vomiting, and rashes, and there is just no other choice but to stay home; your mind drifts at work, often; breast milk leaks during a meeting; and wondering if this all will ever pass.

Two secrets for you, dear women, who are at the beginning of this journey:

First, mothers make the best workers. Who else can plan, manage, multi-task, organize, collaborate, and work for hours on end like we can? You will develop new skills that will make you even better at your current and future jobs just by being a mother. Good employers and supervisors know that.

Second, moments of wonder happen every day as a parent. Sometimes every hour. See them. Laugh or cry about them. They are precious. They are your gift from *your* child. And it all passes . . . fast.

HERE ARE TRACY FINK'S THOUGHTS ON THE POWER OF "KINDFULNESS" AND COMPASSION

It's been a long time since my two now college-aged sons physically needed "their mommy," but the memory of the challenges of when they did is still fresh in my mind. It's kind of like that recurring dream where you miss your final exam. I remember vividly the schedule juggling, the carpools, the leaving work early, the tension with my husband over whose meeting was more important, the groveling to other moms for favors. Of course, there was love, laughter, giggles, and hugs, but looking back, I took those beautiful things for granted while focusing on other things that did not serve me.

Today, I am happy to report from the other side that, while advancing our careers, my husband and I succeeded in raising two productive, kind, slightly-stressed, conscientious, independent kids.

My younger son told me at his recent high school graduation "You were always around, Mom." My heart leapt at those words, and in that moment the guilt, shame, and disappointment in myself vanished.

Since becoming an empty nester, I have focused on developing a loving kindness and mindful meditation practice that I wish I had started when my kids were younger. Looking back, I could have saved myself and my family so much unnecessary drama. It is no secret that they fed off my behavior. That is still true today; however, my behavior is more positive and—quite honestly—my family is happier because I am.

Here are some of the beautiful tidbits I have picked up along the way, which make me a happier person:

1. **We are all beginners.** When I had my first baby, I had never been a working wife and mother before. I never had children and did not know what to expect of them or myself. I never had to follow a school calendar. I didn't know that I should go on the school website and read the "Parent Connect" letters. You catch my drift. We don't know what to do until we fall and someone reaches up and helps us on our way. Sometimes that person is us.

2. **Forgive yourself.** See #1.

3. **Surrender is a sign of strength.** When we "surrender", it is an acknowledgement that we have tried to figure out a situation, and now we are handing it over to a higher power. There is nothing weak about surrendering.

4. **Everything changes.** Just because something happened one way does not mean that it is destined to always be that way. There are so many variables that go into a situation. The chances of them happening the exact same way more than once is

very low. What tends to happen, though, is that we prepare ourselves for a predictable outcome and then we are flustered when things don't go as planned. To illustrate this point, I think of the time when I confronted my son about some not-so-admirable behaviors. I had prepared for "battle"—the argument to combat my son's typical defensiveness. When I called him out on the behavior, he broke down and said he knew it was wrong but had gotten so deep in the weeds he didn't know how to get out. I was stopped in my tracks! We then had a real conversation about what was causing these behavior problems and worked together to find a solution. This incident taught me not to make assumptions and more importantly to keep the lines of communication open. Letting go of expectations and remembering we can always begin again are valuable lessons (in meditation and in life).

5. **Listen to your body.** Our bodies are so smart. When my kids were younger, I wish I had paid more attention to physical signs and had the tools to label feelings without judgment. Sometime what I labeled as anger was really fear. If I just paused, took a moment to listen to what my body was telling me, I could have avoided a lot of misunderstanding.

6. **Keep a gratitude journal.** Each night, take five minutes and write down in your smartphone three things you are grateful for. As you do this, you will begin looking for things in your day to write down,

> and your perspective will begin to shift towards gratitude. It works, I promise.
>
> As a not-so-young mother, I am struck by the power of "kindfulness"—paying attention with compassion and kindness towards yourself and others. It will certainly make me a better grandmother when the time comes—and not too soon I hope!

As you think about the big picture and the long view, mamas, can you recall any other life experiences that have changed your perspective in a drastic way? What new perspectives do you hope motherhood will give you both on life and on work?

MINDFUL MINDSET:
COMBAT BEING OVERWHELMED

In addition to zooming out and focusing on having a broader perspective, another step in the journey to having a "mindful mindset" as a new working parent is learning tools for coping with strong feelings of anxiety and being overwhelmed that can creep into your days.

I have never felt so overwhelmed in my entire life as I was the first few weeks back at work after the birth of my second child. Having a four-month old and a (potty-training) two-year-old at home, a challenging job, food that needed to be cooked, a house that needed cleaned—all on zero sleep—was simply too much. I was doing too much. Absolutely. But, nothing seemed optional and I hit rock bottom every night.

A few months later, after learning to reach out for help and wising up a bit as to what was necessary versus optional in this crazy mama world, I had a conversation with two friends—one who does not have children and one who does—that went something like this:

Friend without kids: My to-do list really gets me down . . . I mean, everything on the list has to get done at *some* point. So I may as well work to find time to do everything.

Friend with kids + me (knowing glances, statement in near-unison): Oh, *no*. Everything on that list does *not* have to get done at some point!

There is no easy answer to how to deal with that sense of being overwhelmed many working mamas feel. (Otherwise, Brigid Schulte wouldn't have a written a brilliant book entitled *Overwhelmed: Work, Love, and Play When No One Has the Time*.) I have, however, learned a few time management and mindfulness strategies that have restored some sanity to my days.

Here are two of my favorites that I incorporate into my life as a working mama:

First, curate your days. (Inspired by Leo Babauta's Zenhabits blog at Zenhabits.net.) What's the first thing that comes to mind when you think of the word *curator*? Yep—a museum. Think of an amazing art gallery and how the work on the walls is so carefully selected and placed. Now think of the museum's entire collection, out of view from the public, and imagine what that storage space looks like. It must be pretty packed and chaotic, right? Now think about what the museum would look like if you took all that artwork and packed the walls with it. Forget white space around each painting. The important thing is every piece of art can be seen! What a beauty! What an impressive museum? Right?! I don't think so . . .

The same holds true for that to-do list of yours. Yes, it is true that some things (packing food for your baby for day care; a shower every now and then, especially if you are going to an office) are not optional. But more things probably are than you are willing to admit. Take those lists, and curate them.

Think about what are your most important work tasks—those that will help you meet your goals and shine as an employee—and select your top three things to get done each day. Focus on those. Do those well. And leave the rest for another art exhibit.

Second, savor your moments. As everything goes whizzing by in a packed working-mama day, it's easy to collapse into bed with nothing but a blur for a memory of what may have happened in the past sixteen hours. While I would love to be able to be in the moment all day, that is simply not possible. If I put my mind to it, though, I can remember to stop, breathe, and sink into a few special moments each day that I'll remember for a long time.

Every morning, I work hard to savor my shower. My husband has the kids, the sound washes out any kid screams, and the cascading water feels like a massage on my back. After work, as I spend time with my kids before we eat, I sink into play for a few minutes and savor the time I have to watch my babies' discoveries. Who knew my one-and-a-half-year-old didn't like playing trains sitting up but with his cheek pressed to the carpet to gaze into the steam engines at eye level? These are now the moments I choose to remember from the day, sink into, and love.

While there are no quick fixes to a mama's being overwhelmed, there are ways to play with time and make it slow down just a bit so you can take in the white space and sink deep into the train set or land of make believe with your kids. In the meantime, you can also cross those never-mind-don't-really-need-to-happen tasks off your daily to-do list.

MINDFUL MINDSET:
ALLOWING YOURSELF YOUR FEELINGS

As Shawn Fink and Coleen Kivlahan described so elegantly, this time in life is full to the brim with such a wide array of human feelings. Some are brand new; some are reminiscent of times past; some are comforting; others are startling.

The important skill in the feelings arena is to get into the practice of naming what you feel and taking the time to sit with those feelings as they arise. My friend, Alexandra Hughes, a coach for overwhelmed mothers, has these words of wisdom on the subject:

HERE ARE ALEXANDRA HUGHES' THOUGHTS ON FEELINGS

Begin connecting, acknowledging, and experiencing your feelings without judgment before baby, and keep at it after baby arrives.

Remember, negative emotions are neither bad nor unhealthy. Not feeling grief after losing something you value (i.e., time with babe) would be unusual and abnormal, just as not feeling anxious about putting something you value on hold (i.e., your professional career) would be.

Identify how your body responds when certain feelings surface, and take the time to breathe into these emotions or the place in your body where they are strongest felt. Sit with your feelings and allow them to flow (even in the form of tears).

Observe yourself with compassion during this journey. A journal or sketchbook documenting this experience is an excellent way to express these emotions and to grow in self-awareness. Cry, swear, and laugh into your journal—let it hold your heart.

Understanding, accepting, and acknowledging your feelings is a first step in self-awareness.

What are three feelings that are coming up for you, mama, in relation to returning to work? What truth do you think they are they telling you about the new you that is emerging?

MINDFUL MINDSET:
MANAGING NEW MAMA ANXIETY

As I began working with more and more new mamas, one topic that came up time and time again was anxiety. Not being a mental health professional myself—but knowing the

Mindful Return community needed some expert advice on this topic—I reached out to Megan Hughes-Feltenberger. Megan is a clinical psychologist and Assistant Professor of Psychology in Psychiatry at Weill Cornell Medicine, who specializes in treating anxiety disorders with cognitive behavioral therapy and is, herself, a new mama. I asked her to weigh in on best practices for managing general stress and anxiety, because the perinatal stage is one known for increasing anxiety symptoms. I love her actionable advice.

HERE ARE MEGAN HUGHES-FELTENBERGER'S THOUGHTS ON MANAGING STRESS & ANXIETY IN NEW MOTHERHOOD

Some people tend to run anxious all the time and others are generally pretty calm and relaxed. With that said, having a baby can really pump up the stress level for anyone. Those last weeks of pregnancy are rough on sleep, it is hard to exercise, and it seems impossible to find time for self-care while scrambling to wrap things up at work and prepare for baby. And, your body is CREATING ANOTHER HUMAN BEING. It can take a toll. Finally, there are so many unknowns during pregnancy, labor, and delivery, the infant stage, and preparing to work, that it is easy to understand why anxiety might increase.

Anxiety can come in many forms. First, it can show up with the types of thoughts you have: increased number of worries, difficulty controlling the amount you worry, and obsessive thoughts that get stuck in your head. Second, you might notice it in things you do when you are anxious: urges to do rituals to clear your head of obsessions (e.g., I should boil those pacifiers again . . . and again . . . and again), lots of asking friends and family for reassurance (e.g., calling three different people to make SURE it is okay that the baby hasn't pooped today). Third, you might experience anxiety more physiologically, in your body, for example through heart racing, sweating, or hyperventilating. Or, it can all come in one big ugly mix. All of it feels pretty lousy.

While all women may notice an increase in stress and anxiety in the perinatal stage, some women will go on to develop perinatal anxiety disorders. They are at least as common as perinatal depression, but they often are not discussed as much. If you notice symptoms of anxiety that cause a significant amount of distress or impairment, check in with your doctor for treatment options.

Websites like ADAA.org (Anxiety and Depression Association of America), ABCT.org (Association for Behavioral and Cognitive Therapies), and IOCDF.org (International OCD Foundation) can give you more information and connect you with clinicians specializing in anxiety disorders in your area. And, of course, if you are experiencing thoughts about death, suicide, or harming yourself or somebody else, do not keep it inside. Go to an emergency room or call 911. We have good treatments for anxiety and depression, and you do not have to suffer alone.

With that disclaimer, if you are noticing an uptick in anxiety and stress, you may want to try a few things on your own to help you feel a bit better:

Use These Skills to Help Calm Those Anxious Thoughts

1. **Recognize the "what if?"** If the sentence starts with "what if . . . . . .", then what follows is anxiety. Don't even bother listening to the rest of the sentence. Or if you can't ignore it, say, "there my anxious brain goes again . . . . . . okay, let's see what my anxiety has come up with this time." Remember: just because you have the thought does NOT mean it is true.

2. **Battle it with humor.** Anxiety likes to be taken very, very seriously. Try using humor to fight it back. Take the anxious thoughts and sing them or use a finger puppet to say them. I know this sounds bizarre, but give it a shot. Somehow, saying, "I'll never finish that work project, I'll get fired, and my whole family will starve!" in the voice of Scooby Doo just makes it seem less horrible.

3. **Play "Best, Worst, Most Likely."** Anxiety has a few other tricks up its sleeve. It focuses on your desire to be *absolutely certain* that everything is going to be okay. But, of course, we can't be certain about

anything in the future. So, the sooner we tolerate uncertainty, the less anxiety we have. To get more comfortable with anxiety, try my favorite trick: a game called, "best, worst, most likely."

When a worry pops into your head, ("what if that weird bump on his face is HERPES and he has HERPES FOREVER!"), first notice your anxiety rising and then jump in with this skill. Remember, go extreme! Your anxiety is doing that anyway, and you want to go even bigger than the anxiety is going.

What's the worst that could happen? He has herpes, it somehow turns into something really dangerous and he is seriously ill, is the laughingstock of all babies everywhere, never gets married, and lives a sad, horrible life.

What is the best that could happen? (Remember, go extreme.) The weird red mark on his face is actually a sign that he has some beneficial gene mutation that will confer incredible intelligence, attractiveness, and mental health. He will be loved by everyone he meets and will live a life full of perfection.

What is most likely? It's a weird mark on his face that will probably go away soon. If it doesn't, you'll show it to the doctor, and s/he'll let you know what next steps you should take to address it. Try it. This skill can really work. And, if it makes you smile while you are going extreme, even better!

4. **Feeling it in your body.** If you get the physiological symptoms of panic or have actual panic attacks, keep in mind that they are physically uncomfortable but are not unsafe. Your heart can beat over 200 beats a minute for weeks before doing itself any damage. A fifteen-minute panic attack, although really unpleasant, is not going to harm you in any way. If you notice your body starting to ramp up, just remind yourself, "okay, these are my anxiety symptoms. My body has reacted as if there is a fire, but I know it's just a false alarm. I just have to wait it out. It will feel uncomfortable, but it will regulate itself in a few minutes."

Change Behavior a Little at a Time

The best way to fight anxiety is to face your fears. You don't have to jump in to your biggest fear, but start with a little step in the right direction. Anxiety feeds off avoidance. The more you avoid something, the more you think you need to avoid it.

Noticing that you are way more germaphobic than you were in the past? Take the subway and touch the seat without using hand sanitizer.

Afraid to drive with your little baby in the car? Start driving on a small, quiet road. Work your way up little by little.

Noticing you do not want to make those phone calls? Make one per day.

Wanting to avoid speaking up in meetings? Give yourself an assignment to speak up once in the next meeting you're in.

Afraid of going in elevators because you might panic? Go on the biggest, safest, easiest elevator with a safety person. Start there, and then get progressively harder.

By starting small and working up, the things you've been avoiding will get easier, and anxiety won't have a chance to take hold.

Take Care of Yourself and Get Physical

Taking care of yourself is SO important to reducing anxiety. I know this is really, really, really hard to do when you don't have any time to yourself anymore. Here are the key things to focus on:

1. **Take help when people offer it.** Learn to say YES to others' offers of help and time. Then give yourself a few moments to take some deep, cleansing breaths. Do a few yoga poses. Listen to a relaxation exercise online. Use a mindfulness meditation app on your phone.

2. **Sleep.** I know, I know. I was there, too! I remember when getting four nonconsecutive one-hour chunks of sleep in 24 hours was the best I was going to get. Those first few weeks are completely insane. But, after that, do your best to get enough rest. I know it is especially hard once you go back to work. My plan was that when I put the baby down at 7 pm, I would get in bed soon after. He would get up three or four times, but at least I was getting his long chunks of sleep when he was, too. I gave up on showering, cooking, and cleaning, but I prioritized

sleep. Figure out who can help, so that you can get as much of your eight hours as possible.

3. **Eat.** I know, this one, too. When is there any time? But, NOW is the time to make sure you are eating healthy, even if that means healthy food is being delivered to your house.

4. **Exercise.** Ha! I know: NO TIME! But, if this means going out on a walk, taking the subway to a further stop and walking the rest of the way, taking the stairs, bouncing your baby on the yoga ball to sleep—just do something. Getting sweaty can be a great way to burn off some anxious energy.

MINDFUL MINDSET:
COMMITTING TO SELF-CARE

"Self-care is never a selfish act—it is simply good stewardship of the only gift I have, the gift I was put on earth to offer to others." — Parker Palmer

What new mom has time for herself? Or even more challenging: what *working* mom has time for herself? What new mom even gets to go to the bathroom by herself for a few moments of peace?!

As a new mom, I certainly didn't. Maternity leave was exhausting, for sure, but while I was on leave with my second baby, I did manage to learn how to sneak in a nap while he napped, and I made it out to baby-and-me yoga class once a week. In the late afternoon, at least I had a few minutes to put dinner together with baby strapped to me in a Moby wrap, before my husband and toddler got home.

When I went back to work, though, there was *zero* margin for me. And I truly mean zero. By the time I got home from work and my husband and I got the kids fed and to sleep, washed all the bottle parts, pump parts, sippy cups, and dishes, and packed food and milk for the next day, I would literally collapse head-first into bed. Without a moment for myself. Without a thought that I might *need* a moment.

I told myself there was just no time for *me*. This craziness would pass at some point, and I would get time for myself one day. In a few months. Or a few years. But not today.

Truth be told, there really wasn't much time for me, no matter how you looked at it. I wasn't going to be able to steal away from work or kids for a relaxing yoga class, a massage, a pedicure, or a date night. It just wasn't going to happen if I was going to keep going to work. Keep the kids rolling out the door to day care each morning. If I was going to get even the minimal amount of sleep one needs to get by.

But if I had it to do over, I would have done a better job getting into good, EASY and FAST micro-self-care habits during my pregnancy and maternity leave that would have made a big difference in my day and in my attitude. I would have incorporated *tiny* routines that would have decreased my number of meltdowns and left me feeling more confident that I could handle these challenges.

What tiny steps are these? Here are some ideas of things I now incorporate into my days that truly make all the difference:

1. **Set a daily intention.** When I first heard about this idea—to set an intention by thinking about how I wanted to feel that day and what I wanted the day to look like (see AbundantMama.com/project-52-how-to-set-a-daily-intention)—I thought, "Great!" "Love it!" "I'll do that every day." And you know what? I didn't. Why? Because I FORGOT. I was so sleep-deprived, I could never even remember to set the intention in the morning. So I came up with an acronym for myself to help me remember.

   Now, every morning when I take a shower, I think "ISS". I = Intention (set one!). S = Stretch (do a yoga pose or two just to stretch and remind myself my body is still there). S = Savor (take a moment to savor the hot water splashing on my face). And of course "is" is a form of "to be," which reminds me to stop *doing* for just one moment and *be*. ISS has saved my sanity.

2. **Take a daily pause.** This was another idea I thought was brilliant but kept forgetting. Until I built it into a daily transition that helped me switch gears. At the end of my day at work, I always switch shoes—from work shoes back into my commuting sneakers for my walk to the metro. I now take a moment while switching shoes to take a deep breath. Do nothing for 30 seconds (a whole minute if I'm feeling daring!) and think about the evening I want to have at home with my kids. It helps me release the day, and gives me at least a moment for myself before I head back home.

3. **Turn your commute into me time.** On days I commute to the office, I do things that make me look forward to—rather than dread—the commute. (1) I read a few pages of a fun book on the metro; and (2) I stop off at a park bench (on nice days) or hotel lobby (if it's cold or raining) and sit quietly for five minutes. I either turn on the Insight Timer app, do a guided meditation, or just focus on breathing. It changes the way I start my workday.

4. **Keep a gratitude journal.** We learned about "finding the good" from Shawn Fink earlier in this chapter. For me, "finding the good" takes the form of a daily gratitude journal. I take five minutes each night before bed to turn on some calming meditation music and write five things I am grateful for. It helps me to take a new look at challenges (yes, I'm exhausted . . . AND my kids are happy and healthy), go to bed in a positive frame of mind, and remember to capture in words those amazing baby experiences and toddler quotes I would otherwise quickly forget.

5. **Use your computer password as a reminder.** I decided to make my computer login not just a combination of random numbers and letters but to make it mean something by including a word that encourages me to calm down. (While still maintaining the appropriate level of security, of course!) Think about a word or phrase that helps you remember to breathe and be present and incorporate it into your password.

I did not learn these techniques until my second child was almost one—long after I had returned from maternity leave twice. If you are doing them already, you are *so* on a good path to having a mindful, nurturing return to work. If you are not, *now* is the time to start wherever you are in your pregnancy, maternity leave, or time back at work. Take *one* baby step right now. Just one. And see what happens.

MINDFUL MINDSET: STARTING A MEDITATION PRACTICE WHEN YOU HAVE NO TIME

I have always been a Type A, need-for-order sort. I am someone who likes structure in my days, prefers to avoid the unexpected, and enjoys planning and knowing what will come next. As anyone who has had a baby knows, though, order goes out the window pretty soon after you bring that bundle of joy home from the hospital. When my second child arrived and I had a toddler and a baby on my hands, any last strand of predictability to my days was snapped in two, got torn to shreds, and became a long-lost dream.

As a working mom, I was having a harder and harder time finding calm in the chaos around me and was grasping for ideas on how I might get my head in a better place. I remembered people recommending meditation to me over the years as a way to find stillness and calm, and truth be told, I had tried some guided meditations and liked them in the past. That was *before* becoming a mom, though, and having NO time for myself whatsoever. How on earth could I pick up a new meditation "hobby" now? Doing *nothing* for some period of time—any period of time!—seemed like a waste of time.

Until I tried it. In tiny, tiny doses. Because that was all the time I had.

First, I had to fight off all those voices that told me I couldn't do this:

You don't have a zafu (a meditation pillow)? Can't start until you get one! Nonsense, I told her. There's a Boppy in the baby's room. Sit on that. And so I did.

Your house isn't quiet! You have nowhere to go to sit and do this. Okay, you win on that one. My house simply is not quiet most days. But that doesn't mean I can't start. So now on my way to work some days, I sit outside on a park bench by a fountain or in a hotel lobby, turn on the fabulous Insight Timer app for five minutes, and away I go. On Fridays I work from home and my house *is* quiet though, so I pull out the Boppy in the baby's room, plop down on the floor, and take my five or ten minutes of calm.

All you have is five minutes! Ha! That's nothing. What good can that do? "Oh sweetie, you have no idea!", I now have to laugh. According to my Insight Timer stats (yes, the app actually has stats . . . it *knows* the Type A side of me likes my metrics!), I've meditated exactly 34% of days over the four past months. And, my average meditation session is exactly 5.3 minutes. So if I wanted to beat myself up and say that's a pathetic record, I easily could. But I don't, because I *feel* the difference. I know my brain has been rewired a bit and that even just five minutes sets my day on a different, calmer track.

This sitting and doing nothing is frivolous! You have a million things to do! And I will get them done faster, better, and in a more relaxed state, if I take this time for me.

My meditation adventure is a work in progress, and I am definitely still a novice. But even these small doses have made all the difference in helping me be present for myself and for those two wonderful and crazy kids of mine.

MINDFUL MINDSET: COMBATING WORKING MAMA GUILT (OR, COMPARISON IS THE THIEF OF JOY)

Ah, guilt. You knew we would get to it eventually, right? And you probably knew that the "g" word might come up for you when you became a mom. It can be hard to predict, though, just how intensely you'll feel the guilt when your little bundle arrives in your life.

Becoming a parent was most definitely *unlike* any other experience I'd had to date. Other than knowing some basics of taking care of kids from my teenage babysitting years and watching (from a safe distance) a few friends and colleagues enter the world of new parenthood, I didn't have much real-life knowledge of how it would go. There was a pretty big gap between the number of internal reference points I had for other tough life experiences and the number of parent-related reference points I could draw on when our first baby arrived.

To fill those gaps, I needed information about how the rest of the world did things like coping with baby reflux. Heading back to work on no sleep. And sterilizing pump parts. So I did the inevitable: I compared what I was doing to how others around me were managing.

Sometimes, these comparisons proved to be really helpful in teaching me new tricks of the trade. Benchmarks can, of course, be useful tools.

But other times, these comparisons served to make me feel pretty crappy: I *was* pretty excited about that four-hour stretch of sleep my baby got . . . until I learned that my friend's son—who is the exact same age—slept 12 straight hours. I *thought* I had returned to being a productive employee. Until I had to miss an important meeting because my baby was sick and all my other colleagues were there. I *thought* my baby was developmentally on track, but a friend's baby was walking by eight months. And when I walked past all my diligent coworkers' offices to get out the door at 4:30 pm to get my baby from day care, I felt like a pretty big slacker.

I am now about six years into the parenting thing, and reframing *unhelpful* comparisons is still a work in progress for me. I have learned, however, to start asking myself how *I* truly feel about something, rather than whether I am on some sort of "right" track or not. Last year, one of the mamas in the Mindful Return E-Course taught me the mantra "comparison is the thief of joy" (apparently a Teddy Roosevelt quote)—which I now remind myself of daily.

Here is my advice:

If guilt leaves you feeling like you're somehow falling "short", remind yourself that "short" is a word that implies a comparison to something else. Then ask yourself: is the comparison to your *own* expectations? If so, perhaps it's time to adjust them, just as everything else in your universe that now involves keeping another human being alive has had to change.

Or, is it the comparison to what "everyone else" is doing, or perhaps what so-called "society" says you should be doing? If so, it's time to turn inward and stop making those other people the yardstick.

As useful as comparisons and benchmarks can be, they should not dictate how we feel about ourselves. A colleague recently lamented to me that despite loving his job, he feels "behind" in his career because he started in one direction, changed paths, and is now a few years older than most of his work peers. I felt compelled to ask him: "What exactly are you 'behind'? On whose schedule?"

Given that comparison may be inevitable, my recommendation is to find some people who inspire you—perhaps on the calm, or balance, or creativity, or daring front—and compare yourself to *them*. *Not* for the purpose of falling short—but for the purpose of learning from them those qualities to which you aspire.

I *do* leave work at 4:30 pm to get my kids nearly every day. And I'm intentionally on a 60% schedule at my law firm. I may not be keeping up with others by some standards, but this pace works for me. To use comparison for good, I now dare to ask: Can I be as thoughtful as she is? As committed to being healthy as she is? As gracious and empathetic as I just saw him be to his team? It is much more fun to be inspired by—rather than feel threatened by—other people, and keeping a close eye on the comparisons you're making can help drive that guilt way down.

MINDFUL MINDSET: THOUGHTS ON GUILT AND PUBLIC POLICY

Valerie Young of Your (Wo)Man in Washington blog fame (Mom-mentum.org/blog/category/woman-in-washington), has some strong feelings about working mama guilt. She is the Public Policy Analyst for Mom-mentum, a non-profit organization providing leadership, education, and advocacy for mothers as they meet today's personal and professional challenges. Valerie is an advocate for recognition of mothers' contributions to our national well-being and is a proponent of economic security and independence for those who care for family members.

HERE ARE VALERIE YOUNG'S THOUGHTS ON THE INTERSECTION OF GUILT AND PUBLIC POLICY

My own return to work 20 years ago was rough. I was a lawyer and had been home with my baby boy for about 10 weeks; some of them paid. I cared very much about my career, and of course, about my husband and son. When my daughter was born four years later, I returned to work again, but gave up after four months of frustration and discouragement, feeling utterly incompetent at everything.

A great deal has changed since then. Millions more mothers have joined the workforce, and some employers put more effort into holding onto established and valued employees after they have children. When my youngest started full-day kindergarten, I started a new career in public policy, and learned about the circumstances surrounding family care work, employment, cultural attitudes, and the economic impact of motherhood on women. Focusing on mother's rights and policy, I now know my struggles had very little to do with me, and a great deal with how little we as a society value family care and the economically-essential unpaid domestic labor performed mostly by women.

My mama's heart aches when I hear another mother express feelings of guilt and inadequacy. In most cases, these feelings are so misplaced. Mothers in the United States don't have many of the social supports taken for granted in other countries. Without realizing how much of an outlier the United States is, mothers assume responsibility for situations over which we have no control. Women are more educated than ever and now make up nearly half the workforce— hugely significant demographic shifts. But there has been only a minimal corresponding shift in workplace cultures, in the amount of care work fathers do, and in our state and federal policies. As a result, mothers are sucking up most of the resulting stress, chaos, and exhaustion that comes from a twenty-first century workforce and mid-twentieth century family policies. Mothers in most states have no right to a single paid day off after giving birth. Some employers offer it, most don't, and even when it is available, it is woefully too short.

Finding and affording child care is handled as a personal problem in this country. Quality varies widely and in 31 states, child care costs as much or more as a year's tuition at a public university. Managing a routine illness or injury—bound to happen at one time or another—easily becomes a family crisis without a comprehensive sick leave policy. Employers are not required to offer it, and when they do, it is often limited to the worker's illness alone. The mother who must take her child to the doctor, or stay home until the flu runs its course, risks not just missing pay but losing her job entirely. Not to mention that on average, women are still making less than men in all job sectors, no matter how high up the ladder they go or how educated and experienced they are. The motherhood penalty, or mommy tax, is very real and well-documented. Men and women doing the same job with similar backgrounds and abilities will find very different challenges at work.

Years of research and analysis have established that mothers face a very steep uphill climb and are, for all intents and purposes, on their own in managing the obligations and expectations of bosses, families, and the harshest critic of all, ourselves. Like any case of injustice, the status quo is painfully slow to change and will not do so voluntarily. Public policy does offer effective solutions and some members of Congress are working towards removing the gender wage gap, making paid family leave available to all workers, and ensuring access to paid sick days and affordable, high-quality child care. Their efforts will never succeed, however, unless mothers and other family caregivers join in with vocal and public support. We have demanded very little of our elected leaders so far and find ourselves (not surprisingly) really underserved by governmental action.

The good news is that we hold the answers to these problems in our own hands. The hands that hold our babies, spoon mashed peas into their mouths, and cover our eyes for peek-a-boo can type an email to our members of Congress, dial the phone so it rings in their office, and touch the screen in the voting booth. The only people who can help us are ourselves.

TO SUM UP THE MINDFUL MINDSET SKILLS:
LEARN TO BE OKAY WITH THE BABY PACE

As a goal-oriented, striving-to-be-less impatient, working mama, the last thing I wanted to hear when I went back to work after maternity leave was that somehow I couldn't do it all. Do it all immediately. And do it all well.

But really, in my heart of hearts, I knew plans had to change. The pace of what I called progress on projects in my life had to change. I knew deep down that slower could mean better. Deeper. Richer. And well-lived.

Before having my first baby and going back to work, there were lots of things I enjoyed doing and managed to find time for, including writing poetry. Then along came my first munchkin. And most non-essentials came to a standstill.

Somehow, when my baby was just under a year old, I managed to eek out this poem about my frustrations. I share it with you to say, "*Yes.* You *can* do those things you loved before you became a mama." In slivers, and tiny bites, and pieces for now, and more later as your kids grow. And that for now, you can simply soak up and love—just love—the moments you are in.

BABY PACE

With baby at home
I don't find time
anymore
to write poems.
My first pen to paper
these ten months
is to write this lament.

But life with baby
IS poetry.
From the gurgling cadence
of his ba ba babbles
to rhymes and sighs and lullabies . . .

Fleeting nuzzles
in my neck;
we clap each other's hands
for patty cake.
Moo ba la la,
the farmer said;

please, please little redhead
let's go to bed!

So my poems
simply
will have to wait.
Words do no justice
to the angel skin
cuddle roo
magic giggles
or Big Love
anyway.

Chapter 3

ALL THOSE LOGISTICS

Now that you have the tools to get your head in a better place for returning to work, we will look at how to tackle all those crazy logistics. Remember: committing to getting yourself organized and learning new mama tricks of the trade can free up your precious brain space to focus on your even more precious baby.

In this chapter, we will explore everything from: consolidating the chaos in your home; transitioning your baby to child care; using your calendar to your advantage; nourishing your baby (pumping and not pumping); putting food on your own table; coping with sick days, snow days, and the land of the unexpected; negotiating for flexibility at work; traveling for work; making the most of your weekends; setting boundaries; learning how to say no . . . and more.

For ease of reading, I have attempted to divide these strategies into those that are more home-based (Part 1: On the Home Front) versus work-based (Part 2: Work Side Logistics of Maternity Leave and Return). This distinction is admittedly arbitrary, as the lines between work and home tend to blur in working motherhood. The chapter concludes with advice on some skills that will serve you well in both parts of your lives (Part 3: Critical Skills for *Both* Work and Home).

PART 1: ON THE HOME FRONT

HOME FRONT LOGISTICS: CONSOLIDATE CHAOS

I hear from working mamas all the time that their days are so scattered. Does the following sound familiar? "I can't seem to find a chunk of time to collect my thoughts in the evenings between packing milk and lunches, paying bills, ordering diapers, filling out day care forms, scheduling appointments... How do I get back some sanity?"

My secret? Consolidate. At our house, we have instituted what we refer to as a "Saturday Basket" that sits on top of our microwave in the kitchen. Into the basket go bills, birth announcements that need a response, forms to fill out, lists of things we need to order, retirement info that needs reviewing, a list of meals for the week. You name it.

Mundane, frequent, and annoying tasks seem to take up *way* less of my emotional energy when they go into the basket, and I love that they are temporarily checked off my to-do list during the week. Being in the basket keeps them from spiraling around in my head!

Then, every Saturday evening, my husband and I have the hottest date ever—what we call our Saturday Meeting. After the kiddos are in bed, we take out the basket, tackle what is inside in one big swoop, and go through a checklist that includes:

- Bills and money

- Anything we need to order

- Planning out our week (including who could take kids if they get sick)

- Scheduling weekend activities (and preserving a few weekend days per month with NO commitments)
- Getting our parents' helper on the books
- Scheduling a monthly date night
- Carving out time for exercise during the week
- Making sure each of us is getting time alone and with friends
- Reviewing our respective business goals

Do we make it through the entire list every week? Nope. But the meeting is still always worth it.

BONUS: ANNUAL PLANNING DAY (A.K.A. THE SATURDAY BASKET ON STEROIDS)

For the past several years, my husband and I have kicked our Saturday Meeting concept up a notch and scheduled an Annual Planning Day, when we cover lots of important topics that will set us up to have a great year ahead. Note that we usually do this in late December with an additional one-day mini-retreat to follow in the middle of the summer. What do we do during this session?

1. **Wordstorm.** So much fun! The very first thing we do is throw out about 15-20 words that describe how last year felt to us. We also brainstorm 15-20 words that describe how we want next year to be. Then we circle three or four of them and continue our planning day with those in mind.

2. **Pull out the calendar.** Look at the year as a whole. A few things we focus on include:

   › Marking all day care/school closure dates and figuring out who will stay home, what backup care we will need, etc.

   › Choosing our children's birthday party dates (and then communicating those to the family).

   › Choosing housecleaning dates for the whole year (and then communicating those to our cleaning service).

   › Scheduling a few date nights (and texting our baby-sitters to check their availability).

3. **Size up travel holistically.** Figure out for yourself how much family travel is too much and how much is just right.

   › If you went on five long car trips to see family last year and that felt like too much, make a commitment to going only three times this year. Then pick the dates and communicate with family about them.

   › Dream about—and start planning for—vacations. Brainstorm together, think big, think realistically, work out budgets, and get excited!

4. **Money, money, money.** ABBA, anyone? Yes, this meeting is a good time to open those bank apps, see what is in there, and set goals for the coming year.

   › Do you have specific savings goals in mind? Have you created a separate savings account for each goal?

We use CapitalOne360, formerly known as ING, and we literally have an account called "Kid Birthday Parties," and another called "Holiday Money," to which we contribute every pay period.

> Think about taxes. Did you pay enough as the year went on so you don't owe a big chunk at the end of the year? If not, can you make a change for this coming year? Will a maternity leave or other time off affect what you owe? Schedule a separate tax prep day sometime before April.

> Talk through those longer-term goals, like kids' college funds (the so-called 529 funds) and your own retirement. How much are you putting aside? Are you on target?

5. **Push the "reset" button on health and exercise.** It is never too late to start again, right? Wherever we find ourselves in December, whether with healthy eating, weight targets, or exercise, January always offers a fresh page. Talk about what you have in mind and agree to be one another's accountability partners.

Yes, it is a lot of ground to cover in one day. You can take periodic breaks. Perhaps do the session at a coffee shop that has good WiFi, go out for a yummy lunch together, and call the day a date.

HOME FRONT LOGISTICS: BLOCK TIME ON YOUR CALENDAR NOW TO ENSURE CALM LATER

I remember well how hard it was—both while pregnant and in the early days of having a baby—to think much past the next day or next major event. When I was pregnant with my first, I (for good reason!) couldn't even imagine what life would be like once he arrived, so I found it difficult to plan for post-baby life. Then, after he was born, simply surviving the days and nights took all the energy I had in the world. Forget planning ahead months and months.

Going through the having-a-baby-and-returning-from-maternity-leave thing one time made me wiser the second time around. These days, I think much more about how if something is not on a calendar, it simply does not happen. I also know how important it is to my own state of calm and sanity to block days and weekends for doing absolutely nothing.

Here are a few ideas for how to take control of your calendar, even before your baby gets here:

1. **Block the first few weekends after your return to work.** The first days of returning to work and having someone else watch your baby are exhausting and emotionally draining. I expected to be tired, but I don't think I anticipated how wiped out my baby would be, too. It is a good idea to keep those first few weekends after your return to work completely clear to take care of yourself, regroup, and reconnect with your munchkin.

2. **Put pump-holds on your work calendar.** If you are planning to breastfeed, it is never too early to put some pumping "holds" on your work calendar for your return. Well before I returned to the office, I put three half-hour holds on my calendar—one in the morning, one around lunch, and one in the mid-afternoon—to reserve time for pumping. With my first baby I needed to pump that many times a day to keep up my supply, but with my second, I only needed to pump twice a day. Having blocked that lunchtime pumping session made me feel like I had some bonus breathing time!

3. **Plan vacations around your child care calendar.** Are there certain days of the year when your day care will be closed? Or when your nanny will be out of town? Find out as soon as you can what the yearly calendar is and schedule yours around it. My day care is closed the entire last week of August. Guess when we go on vacation . . .

4. **Consider a post-baby no fly zone.** Everyone has a different approach to how many visitors they'd like to see and when upon baby's arrival. My husband and I decided we wanted some time alone with our first before the onslaught of friends and relatives, so we blocked a "one week no fly zone" post-baby. People were allowed to drop off food at our door and leave, but nothing more. It worked out well for us and I would not have traded it for anything. The key here was setting expectations in advance so well-meaning baby adorers did not get offended. (If they got offended anyway, well, I had no control over that.)

Blocking the calendar seems to be a muscle that gets stronger and stronger for me as I keep doing it over time. Now that my kids are little older, I am able to block time for a weekly yoga class and my husband blocks exercise time on his calendar. We plan in advance and commit to a monthly date night and block time for our annual planning meetings.

From what I can tell, blocking time on the calendar in advance never hurts. You can always take those holds off the calendar later if you don't need them, but it's harder to get the time back if someone else managed to grab it from you.

So block that calendar now. Your calmer self will thank you later.

HOME FRONT LOGISTICS:
PUTTING FOOD ON THE TABLE

It was about two months after my second child was born. I was home on maternity leave (past the point of adrenaline being able to mask my ridiculous fatigue), and I had my baby in a sling while I scrambled to put some dinner together before my husband brought our toddler home from day care. I lifted up the lid to my favorite kitchen appliance, our rice cooker, and dumped in a cup of rice. Splash. As soon as I heard the grains hit metal instead of the bottom of the bowl, I cringed. In my sleep-deprived fog, I had forgotten to put the rice cooker bowl back into the machine, and the grains went right into the gears. Bye bye rice cooker. (I learned online that you could in fact send it back to the company for repair, but that cost as much as buying a new one.)

I shed a few tears both at the loss of my dinner plans and at losing a wedding present (and let's be honest, plenty of things other than a ruined rice cooker were making me cry back then anyway . . .). But in doing research into a replacement rice cooker, I discovered the kitchen appliance that would become my new best friend in my scramble to feed the family: the rice cooker/SLOW COOKER/steamer/oatmeal maker. I have precious little counter space, so this four-in-one combo sounded like a dream. And it is. I use at least one function of it almost every day of the week.

There are plenty of places you can turn to for advice on feeding your family quickly and healthily—friends, recipe books, and oodles of websites. I am no great chef or food connoisseur, and my standards in the kitchen are not particularly high. What I do know, however, is that you need to nourish yourself to have energy to nourish your baby, families need to eat (often!), and juggling food preparation with working and caring for children is HARD. Everyone has her own system of getting the job done at a level she's comfortable with—or at least can survive on—and there are tips to be shared to make the burden a bit lighter.

Here are a few I have heard and borrowed:

- Rely on your slow cooker. I try to make one meal in there on a weekend that will last at least two or three days.

- Cook for the week on the weekend.

- Cook meals and freeze them; even cooked pasta freezes.

- Purchase the services of a company that assembles or delivers meals all ready to be cooked. (We are big fans of Blue Apron. There's prep required, which I do on the weekend, but it makes for quick and healthy meals during the week.)

- Buying precut veggies is not cheating.
- Try a meal-planning app like Cook Smarts, Paprika, or Plan to Eat.
- Take out and order in.
- When friends ask what they can bring the baby or how they can help out, say: "The baby's all set, but I could really use a meal or two."

I admit I have had more than one meltdown about what was going to be on the table in a given week, so to save my sanity, I started taking an approach of just letting it go. Whatever I am able to cook on the weekend is fine. If I am not able to cook on the weekend, it is fine. If my husband whips up some nuggets and a salad, that is fine. Whatever it is, we are doing our best, trying to be healthy, and not letting meal stress get us down. When the kids are older, perhaps we'll sharpen our knives again and engage in more culinary experiments. For now, though, I will live with a lower standard and delight in snapping some photos of ketchup on my little guy's face.

HOME FRONT LOGISTICS: THE IMPORTANCE OF BREAKFAST FOR WORKING MAMAS

Dinner is not the only meal worth thinking hard about as a working mama. For advice on *starting* our days on the right foot, I reached out to Marva Makle, an inspiring Ayurvedic health coach who focuses on helping "worn out, burnt out" (WOBO) women. Here is her advice to you working mamas about why you might be hitting that mid-morning wall.

HERE ARE MARVA MAKLE'S THOUGHTS ON STARTING YOUR DAY RIGHT

You dragged your butt out of bed after getting up several times in the night to feed the baby. You're back to work and cranking away on a deliverable that's due in two hours. Suddenly, around 10:30 am, Bam! You hit a wall. No focus, no energy, all you want to do is stare out the window.

Hmm . . . what did you eat for breakfast?

I can hear you now, "Breakfast? Are you kidding? I don't have time for breakfast." As I'm sure you've heard, breakfast is the most important meal of the day. It's the meal that should supply at least a third of the macro and micronutrients your body needs to run without a hitch. You've already fasted overnight, and your body and mind are in desperate need of nutrition.

If you are a woman who is breastfeeding, the need for a quality breakfast is even greater. Given you need an additional 300-500 calories per day while breast-feeding, skipping or skimping on breakfast can easily create a serious energy deficit. With the demands of your schedule, it is quite likely you won't be able to recover from that deficit all day after missing your morning recharge.

Think about what you are eating each morning to "break the fast" and properly fuel your day.

A cup of coffee gulped down on the go? A cup of sugary yogurt or a bowl of "healthy" cereal eaten at your desk? A donut from the break room? Nothing at all?

You deserve so much better than that, and your body and mind NEED more!

When you eat a good breakfast, your day is much more likely to go smoothly. No growling stomach, low blood sugar shakiness, or wandering attention to keep you from nailing those big goals you've set for yourself.

What Breakfast is Right for You?

One of the best—and most fun—ways to find out which foods serve YOU most powerfully is something called the Breakfast Experiment. For one week, eat a different breakfast each day. Record in a notebook what you ate, how you felt immediately after the meal, and how you felt again two hours later.

- Day 1: scrambled eggs or tofu
- Day 2: bean soup or a bean salad
- Day 3: oatmeal
- Day 4: boxed breakfast cereal with milk
- Day 5: muffin and coffee

- Day 6: fresh fruit

- Day 7: fresh vegetables

Feel free to repeat the experiment for another seven days with different foods each morning. Which breakfasts made you feel energized? Which ones didn't? After the experiment, try adding in more of the foods that made you feel great. This is one simple step you can take on your wellness walk.

For links to some fantastic breakfast recipes Marva recommends to start your day on a well-nourished foot, go to MindfulReturn.com/breakfast.

HOME FRONT LOGISTICS: TRANSITIONING YOUR BABY TO CHILD CARE

Whether you have been home on maternity leave for a few weeks or a few months, transitioning your baby to child care can be daunting and fraught with lots of emotions. The day I dropped off my first baby at day care—a place I had researched carefully and truly loved—I left with eyes full of tears, head swimming with thoughts like: "I don't even know these people! . . . My baby! . . . What on earth possessed me to walk out that door?!"

And also, "Hallelujah! For the next few hours, the mysteries behind his cries are someone else's to figure out! His spit-up is someone else's to clean! They are experts at this. I don't even know what the heck I'm doing . . . "

And of course: "Is leaving him for two hours worth

pumping or should I not pump and just wait until I see him? Maybe he won't want to drink any milk at day care and then he'll be hungry? Or maybe he'll drink so much at day care and won't want to nurse that I'll be engorged when I see him?! . . . " What a morning that was.

While that swell of thoughts and emotions is, I suspect, inevitable, the following can help this important transition go more smoothly:

1. **Use a transition week schedule to ease both of you into the experience.** No matter what type of child care arrangement you will be using, ask for an official transition week during which the amount of time in child care increases as the week goes on. I was lucky in that my day care had a schedule they used for all new arrivals, no matter what age of the child, which looked something like this: Monday, 9–11 am, Tuesday, 9 am–12:30 pm, Wednesday, 9 am–1 pm, Thursday, 9 am–3:30 pm, Friday, 9 am–5 pm.

   If you are able to do the transition week the week *before* you start back to work, all the better. For both of my children, I did the transition before returning to the office and I discovered it was much-needed time for me to shop for some non-maternity work clothes, take a yoga class (alone!), have lunch with a friend, and get a haircut.

2. **Don't linger. Last big hug and kiss goodbye, and then go.** I remember my day care teachers telling me it was important not to linger at drop-off, even the first day and the first week. And I remember being really angry at

that warning. "I'll stay as long as I want, thank you very much!" I thought to myself. But, I followed their advice, and I do now believe it is better for the child not to have a really extended goodbye and not to set up an expectation that there will be one, even from the beginning.

3. **Know that baby's sleep "schedule", including night-time sleep, will probably be off for a bit.** I use "schedule" loosely here, as some babies have one from the get-go, and for others, well, there is no such thing. You should expect, however, that whatever you previously had gotten used to is likely to change in the sleep department when child care starts. Baby might get up more at night to cuddle, and it may take a few weeks to get naps figured out. Just remember how quickly everything changes with these little guys. At three months, they still may take four naps a day, but by about the one-year mark, they are down to only one—which always seemed fascinating and crazy to me at the same time.

4. **Plan for extra cuddle time.** Chances are, you will both be extremely happy to see one another at the end of each day—whether you were separated for a few hours or the whole day. At least for your first week back at work, forget the laundry, order in some food, clean only the bottles you will need for the next day, and spend some serious time together after work in your favorite snuggle spot.

5. **Remind yourself that "alloparents" have been critical to child rearing for pretty much all of human history.** I learned the term "alloparents" from Brigid Schulte's

Book, *Overwhelmed.* Here is a good introduction to the idea. Note that Brigid is interviewing Sarah Blaffer Hrdy, an evolutionary anthropologist, and they are discussing Kung women in the Kalahari Desert in Africa, 2,000 years ago:

"The whole idea that mothers stayed at camp and the men went off to hunt? No way! These women were walking thousands of miles every year with their children. Or if it was not safe, they were leaving them back at camp." She pauses to drive that point home: "Sometimes mothers left their children back at camp. The children were with their fathers, older siblings, grandparents, relatives, and other trusted, nurturing adults- people Hrdy calls 'allo-parents' ('allo' means 'other than' in Greek). "It's natural for mothers to work. It's natural for mothers to take care of their children," she says. "What's unnatural is for mothers to be the sole caretaker of children. What's un-natural is not to have more support for mothers."

6. **Pause at transition time and take care of yourself.** Take the time—whether one minute or five—to be mindful of the transitions in your day—from baby to work, and work to baby. To help me shift gears with intention, I try to pause during my metro commute. I take a minute to breathe in my workday and breathe out my work to-do list. Then I breathe in the thought of the babes who await on the other side of my metro ride, and I breathe out however I am feeling about having been gone. Take note of how you're feeling and just *feel.* Take care of yourself

your first weeks back—and every week thereafter. To help in this taking-care-of department, make an effort to find other mamas who have been there, done that, and talk to them about their experiences.

Finally, just breathe, mama, breathe. This transition will sort itself out. You will be fine. Baby will be fine. And each day will bring you a reunion to cherish.

HOME FRONT LOGISTICS: BABY FIRSTS DON'T EXIST UNTIL YOU SEE THEM

One of the essential chapters in the guilt book that so many new working mamas carry around with them seems to be the one entitled "I'm sad and guilty that because I'm working, I'm going to miss my baby's milestones." You know, those first claps, rolls over, crawls, steps . . .

I certainly had this thought before I had my first child, and I've seen it come up time and time again with the amazing and strong mamas who have taken the Mindful Return E-Course.

The feeling didn't surprise me, given that I had experienced it myself . . . but the sheer volume of women who have said this to me since I started Mindful Return really startled me. I also think I was startled because after giving birth to my first baby, this fear was absolutely a nonissue for me. It was one I hadn't given another thought to for years.

Why, I wondered, hadn't "missing firsts" turned out to be a problem for me? *Was it that I was too overwhelmed to notice that I'd missed these things?* Nope. *Or that I simply didn't care?*

Wrong again. It was that the pure joy I felt at seeing my son clap or pull himself up or walk for the first time instantly erased any idea that he may have done it before. Oh, and the fact that my day care simply didn't tell me when a milestone had occurred didn't hurt either.

My advice to new mamas who are going back to work after maternity leave is this:

- If you are worried about missing milestones, consider asking your child care provider not to tell you that they happened.

- Remind yourself that this issue really is *not* about whether you work outside the home or not. Simply put, it is impossible (not to mention probably unhealthy and undesirable) to spend every single hour of every single day staring at your child. Your baby *will* do new things when he is in the other room with your partner . . . or alone in her crib at night . . . or while you are out on a run . . . or when your back is turned. You know the saying, "if a tree falls in a forest and no one is there to hear it, does it make a sound?" This much is inevitable.

- Repeat after me this great mantra one of my colleagues shared with me: "A baby first doesn't exist until you've seen it!" And keep repeating it.

- When you do see that milestone, celebrate! Jump up and down. Grab your camera and take pictures. Videos. Send them to your friends. Call your family. And be present— truly and completely present—to that amazing moment you have just shared with your little one. I promise you this WILL be the first time your baby gets to witness *your* joy and pride reflected back to him.

I remember going into day care one day sooo excited to tell everyone that my son had started clapping the night before. I got a knowing smile from one of his day care teachers that she had seen it before, but I didn't care. My baby was *clapping*. And how cool was that?!

BONUS WORKING MAMA SECRET:
DAY CARES CAN BE LOBBIED

If you live in a place where demand for quality day care centers is extremely high and space in those centers is extremely low, you know the angst that comes with trying to get a spot for your baby at the time you need it. I live in one of those cities (Washington, DC), and having heard about the crazy scene, began my research on the topic even before I got pregnant. I started a Word document for all of my options and then sent applications and wait list deposits to all of the centers on my list the day I got a positive pregnancy test. (They were in stamped envelopes, waiting to go. Crazy, I know.)

Like many things in this world, though, I advise that you don't sit idly by, waiting to crawl up to the top of those enormous day care waitlists. Yes, mama, day cares can be lobbied.

While I was pregnant, my husband and I toured each center, picked our top choice, and then worked hard to make sure they *knew* they were our first choice. We sent a handwritten thank you after the tour. We sent them a letter announcing the arrival of our little redhead when he was born, and then my husband called every few weeks to check in. (Note: we suspected they got so many calls from new mamas that we bet on my husband's male voice to stand out from the crowd.)

This isn't just my experience. When I interviewed Nedra Pickler (Managing Director at the Glover Park Group and former AP journalist covering the White House) a few months ago, she said the same thing. When you're on maternity leave, "You need to work those waitlists like a job and network," says Pickler. "Those things are not really run in order and can be kind of a racket—the order of admission is totally up to the staff. I would go on tours to meet as many members of the staff as I could and check in regularly with the director. I made sure they knew I would be an involved parent and would bring them a deposit check the moment they had an opening."

For all the day cares we did not lobby, we eventually got into all of them . . . somewhere between one and three years later.

HOME FRONT LOGISTICS: WEEKENDS— RECLAIMING THOSE PRECIOUS 48 HOURS

For new parents, the state of the weekend can come as a bit of a shock. My friend and insightful mama, Arielle Mir, shares some fabulous advice here on how to reclaim that precious time.

HERE ARE ARIELLE MIR'S THOUGHTS ON RECLAIMING YOUR WEEKENDS

Everyone tells you that life after baby is going to be hard. Everyone tells you that "nothing is the same again." I, for one, found those statements tremendously unhelpful, especially because they often lacked specificity about what exactly would be hard and what exactly would change.

When my son was born, one of the biggest changes I did not anticipate was what would happen to my weekends. I knew that having an infant would preclude much of the late night carousing, but who was I kidding? I had abandoned that long before I was pregnant.

But weekends were so much more than that. Pre-baby weekends were pure relief and pure possibility. I could almost always rest and accomplish as much as I needed and maybe even squeeze in a pedicure and breakfast with the ladies.

As overwhelming as those first weeks can be, having a new baby at home was also a bit of a break from our regular routine. We didn't have much family to help, but we had a freezer full of food that kind friends had sent and a sense that all we needed to do was nurture our son and help me recuperate from the delivery.

Saturdays, Tuesdays, who cares? All we did every day was nurse, diaper change, swaddle, repeat.

Fast-forward a few months to when the newborn supports faded away. My partner and I both went back to work, and we had to go back to "normal." That's when our weekends began to feel like pure misery. We couldn't "sleep when the baby sleeps" because when the baby slept—those paltry 40-minute naps that took about as long to settle him—were populated with attempts to grocery shop, scrub the bathrooms, welcome visitors, prep food for the week, catch up on bottle washing . . . the list goes on.

The only way we managed to get anything done was for one of us to take the baby out for a walk and the other to furiously shop/scrub/prep inside the house. We were exhausted ('cause baby doesn't know that weekends are for sleeping in) and resentful of, well, pretty much everything. I cried when I would see families all together at the park or for brunch. How were they doing it all?

Here's the secret: They weren't. No one does. They were making choices . . . tradeoffs. When you become a parent, you have a whole new set of roles and responsibilities that can crowd out your other weekend activities, if you let them, or want them to. One option is to simply let things go. Maybe the bathroom doesn't need to be scrubbed every week. Or maybe it does for you. Only you know what your priorities are.

The bottom line is that "doing it all" in 48 hours is impossible and attempting to do so is a recipe for exhaustion and desperation. Weekends are still the time we have to recharge and reconnect with our families before we do it all again on Monday. With that in mind, here are a few tips for taking your weekends back:

- Ask yourself what you can outsource. Pay someone to clean your house. Get your groceries delivered through a grocery delivery service. Hire a dog walker.

- When you're with your family, be with your family. Take a walk, have a picnic, or go listen to some music. Turn off your phone, forget about the dishes in the sink for a few hours, and really do it. You may find you actually GAIN energy from something like that.

- Treat your date nights like a 401k. Hire your baby-sitter for a specific night or nights each month. Remove the mental cost of having to decide when you and your partner are going to go out.

These were my family's game changer moves, but yours might be different. Whatever you do, know that you are not alone. Every mama and papa all over the world is making choices to help bring a bit more peace to their homes.

HOME FRONT LOGISTICS:
THE WONDERS OF A PARENTS' HELPER

After having a baby and heading back to work, just as Arielle noted, I found that my previously bliss-filled weekends became even more stressful than my workweek. I had a million and one things I needed (or at least thought I needed) to get done at home, I wanted to spend quality time with my little one and my husband, and I wound up angry, frustrated, and exhausted with the inability to get it all done. In the early days of having a baby, those 48 hours were gone before I could blink, and I couldn't seem to catch up.

One of the best decisions my husband and I ever made was to take family friends up on their offer to have their then 12-year-old daughter come to our house as a parents' helper on weekends. She started coming shortly after we had our second child, when "chaotic" did not even begin to describe the state of our household. ("Desperate" might be a more accurate word choice.)

She started coming about two Saturdays a month, from 10 am to 1 pm, which may not sound like much, but made a HUGE difference in our lives. At first, having her there simply freed up one parent to do one or two household chores that wouldn't have gotten done otherwise. Gradually, though, as the kids came to trust her and she grew in her child care experience, we were both freed up to get more done.

We have taken her grocery shopping with us. She has helped out with swimming lessons. She has come over during day care closure days. She has even accompanied us to the zoo and the County Fair. And our kids absolutely, positively adore her.

Here are three benefits you can get from a parents' helper:

1. You get more done at home which frees you up to relax a bit more on weekends.

2. You are still in the house, so you get to spend time with your kiddos and monitor the helper's evolving caretaking skills.

3. They are affordable, enthusiastic, and they grow up into independent babysitters who know and truly love your little ones.

In addition to getting extra help, the other strategy we started employing was to limit our weekend-scheduled activities to one. Yes, just one. We were able to ease up on this as the kids got older, but in the early days, saying no to many a potential commitment helped us focus on one another and survive . . . at least until Monday morning.

HOME FRONT LOGISTICS: HOW A POSTPARTUM DOULA CAN HELP WITH YOUR RETURN TO WORK

A postpartum what? Before I created Mindful Return, I was clueless about so many of the birth professionals who can help a woman's transition to motherhood go more smoothly. Yes, I already had two kiddos of my own, but clearly I had missed out on a vast network of support I could have taken advantage of when my babies were tiny. In part, I was stubborn and had a go-it-alone attitude. In part, I just was not aware of what was out there.

In a world where so many of us live far away from family and close friends, support from experts like postpartum doulas can make all the difference when our little one arrives home. I'm happy to introduce to you Nikki Wray of Metropolitan Doulas, LLC, a Washington, DC-area postpartum doula agency, who explains how you might consider engaging with a postpartum doula to help you with your transition back to work after maternity leave.

HERE ARE NIKKI WRAY'S THOUGHTS ON POSTPARTUM DOULAS

You just had your baby! You made it through the birth you had been anxiously awaiting for months. You made it through weeks of sleep deprivation (more or less in one piece . . .). Now you've survived the dreaded six-week growth spurt, and all of a sudden the end of your maternity leave is looming.

Whether you're a first-time mother or a veteran of multiple pregnancies, one of the most challenging aspects of the postpartum period is navigating your return to work while continuing to juggle all the ongoing responsibilities of caring for your new baby.

Your to-do list probably looks something like this:

- Figure out how to pump at work
- Try on all of your pre-pregnancy work clothing and see what fits
- Work out how to get to the office on time; not covered in spit-up
- Learn how to safely store milk, how to send it to day care each day, and figure out how much to send

- Somehow do all of this while caring for your new, amazing baby . . .

But you don't have to tackle these tasks alone, mama. If your first reaction was the same as Lori's, "a post-partum what?" read on.

Postpartum doulas are baby care experts who can help you with all aspects of newborn care, house-hold organization, and family adjustment, to guide you through all of the many transitions that happen as you welcome your new baby into your family. From answering your many questions about your baby's feeding, sleep, fussiness, patterns, and cues, to giving you hands-on practical help when you most need it, their job is to ease your burden in every way they can.

They are the extra set of hands you wish you had.

They are your own personal Google search; one who has already sifted through all of that contradictory advice for you.

They are professionals you can trust to watch your baby for a couple of hours so you can get things done or take some time for self-care, without worrying that they might put your baby down to sleep on their stomach or introduce rice cereal at 10 weeks old "so baby will sleep better."

Having a postpartum doula in your home can be ex-tremely helpful in ensuring that you feel prepared for your return to work. Perhaps you don't feel ready to leave your baby just yet and you're anxious or scared. Perhaps you are excited to be able to finally leave the house by yourself, yet this leaves you with "mommy guilt." Perhaps you are simply feeling overwhelmed at all there is to tackle with only so many hours in a day. The transition is always challenging, but there are people out there who can support you.

Postpartum doulas can offer guidance and emotional support for this period, hearing your feelings and concerns while helping you tie everything together into a plan that you feel good about.

They can also be the friendly set of hands to hold your fussing baby while you try clothes on for the office, answer questions about pumping and milk storage, and take care of light housework to keep everything flowing while you prepare for your first days back.

To learn more about the role a postpartum doula can play in bringing baby home and preparing for your return to work or to find a postpartum doula in your area, check out DONA International at DONA.org.

HOME FRONT LOGISTICS: SICK DAYS, SNOW DAYS, AND THE LAND OF THE UNEXPECTED

Sick days, snow days, parent-teacher conferences . . . on these days, it's easy to feel like the universe is conspiring against all your best efforts to be a diligent employee. I'll be honest: these are the days I just want to scream my lungs out, pull out my hair, and run far away from my house. Alone. I find there to be nothing more frustrating than feeling like you really, really should be in two places at the exact same time. And yet you can't.

My husband and I have a joke that every night, both of us go to sleep never knowing if we're going to be able to go to work the next day. We love our day care, but we call our kids' classmates their fellow petri dishes. As all parents know, there's no shortage of germs on any playground. And that whole thing about kids' immune systems becoming so incredibly strong through illnesses isn't reassuring when you're trying to figure out who will go pick up the barfing child.

I had a particularly tough run with my youngest—who had seven ear infections in six months—before we went the route of the miraculous ear tubes. A recent winter was tough, too, with seven days home from work just for snow. (Which would have been great fun, if my colleagues without children hadn't continued working remotely and expected everyone to be on teleconferences all day.)

The big issue for me in all this, and I suspect for other responsible parents and employees, is guilt. Guilt that I'm not giving 100% to my job at that moment. Guilt when I'm not the one staying home with our child that day. Guilt that I'm not 100% focused on caretaking, when I *am* the one staying home. I'm a planner by nature and I love order and predictability. Sigh. These are clearly characteristics completely out of sync with parenthood. (Okay, and with life in general.)

Ultimately, there are two things that have gotten me through this constant state of anticipating the unexpected: planning and gratitude. On the planning front, during the Saturday Meeting I discussed earlier in this chapter, my husband and I sit down and talk about who is in the best position to take sick duty on any given day of the coming week. We've had to negotiate and listen fully and deeply to one another's priorities, but we've been able to strike a good balance between us.

Focusing on gratitude also grounds me and helps me see what is really important in the big scheme of things. I am grateful that my little ones are usually healthy. Grateful that I have someone with whom I can share the burden and angst of the unexpected. Grateful that my taking a day off to care for my sick child won't cause me to lose my job. Grateful that the day off is a bigger deal to me than to my team. And grateful that I have had bosses who have been understanding.

My advice is simply this: take a deep breath, and roll—or tumble—into the Land of the Unexpected. Know it is a place populated with parents just like you. And know that sometimes, you can find magical mommy moments in your unexpected time together.

I share with you here, a poem I wrote on one of that winter's many, many snow days:

SNOW DAY

A snowstorm's leftovers
spoiled my plans
to sit in a quiet office today,
attacking assignments
like a honey badger.
Who knew parents
stayed home on snow days?

But I had Remote Desktop—
technology to transport me
to my deadline—
and a Daddy to take the boys
while I worked.

And I witnessed the magic
of eleven-month-old empathy –
"Bup, bup, bup!" babbled Sawyer,
grinning to quell his big brother's tears.

And I plopped down in the snow
in ancient purple snow pants
to make my first snow angel in decades—
Chayse's first of his life.
Oh, and yes. There were toddler tantrums.
Mommy meltdowns. And nonexistent naps.
Of course.

HOME FRONT LOGISTICS: GETTING OUT THE DOOR IN THE MORNING (WITH ONE PAIR OF ADULT HANDS)

Note: this section was originally published on an awesome website you should all explore called Working Moms Against Guilt, found at WorkingMomsAgainstGuilt.com.

Mornings before kids seemed so blissful—in retrospect. You could wake up with just as much or as little time as you needed to perform morning rituals that made your heart sing. Push the snooze button. Or at the very least ensure a shower in time to make it to work. There was predictability, the birds chirped, the sun shone, and . . . well, the rest is a foggy memory for me now.

If you have lived a minute with a baby at home, you don't need me to tell you what weekday morning life is like post-baby. I haven't set a morning alarm since having my first son almost six years ago (those cherubs certainly do not come with snooze buttons), and the tasks required to leave the house have multiplied a hundredfold. Just getting everyone where they need to go in the morning (my youngest to day care, my oldest to school, me to the office) feels like one big game of chess, where all the pieces have come alive and keep walking away on their own. Or at least screaming.

This getting-ready-for-work thing is hard enough with two pairs of adult hands in the house. But subtract one parent from the mix for whatever reason—work travel, early morning meetings, you name it—and suddenly I hear the voice of my son saying in a robotic voice, "Red alert, red alert! Danger, danger!" (Note: I have the utmost admiration and respect for single parents and others who do this single-handedly every morning. You are my heroes.)

When I've done the morning routine solo and actually *did* have to get to work on time, my mantra has been plan, plan, plan—down to every last detail—and maximize what you do the night before.

Here are some strategies that have worked for me:

1. **The Night Before:**

- **Get breakfast ready.** A mama's gotta eat. And while I was nursing, I would always wake up starving. For me, this means literally pouring cereal into a bowl, covering it with tinfoil, and putting it with a spoon on the dining room table. Cutting up fruit I can dump on the cereal in the morning, and putting that in a container in the fridge. And putting morning vitamins out on the table with the cereal and spoon.

- **Put non-perishable baby supplies and anything you need for work by the door** (if you're commuting by foot) **or *directly into your car.*** Diapers, wipes, clothing changes, pump bags, etc. can all be bagged up and ready to go.

- **Pack perishable baby items like milk and baby food into their cooler bag and put that bag in the fridge.** All you need to do in the morning is add the ice packs.

- **Pull out clothes—yours and baby's.** Look up the following day's weather the night before and have outfits for both of you out and ready to go.

- **Shower** so you can wake up and not have to worry about the time it takes to get clean.

2. **The Morning Of:**

- **Set an alarm.** If you're past the point where you are only alive because you are able to sleep every single minute the baby sleeps (and I've been there, so ignore this point if you're not there yet), set an alarm for 10 or 15 minutes before baby usually wakes up. This can give you a jump-start on at least washing your face.

- **Feed baby while you are eating.** I usually just nursed baby while eating that pre-planned bowl of cereal.

- **Hair up!** With long hair, a braid, clip, or ponytail has always been a necessity for me.

Mantras for When Things Go Haywire:

› I have figured out ridiculously challenging things before.

› I am not likely to be fired if I am a few minutes late.

› The world will not end if I forget something today.

› No matter what happens, I am enough.

› Breathe, mama, breathe.

If your little one is still tiny, remind yourself that at least he can't run away from you yet, or tear her socks and shoes off every time you put them on. That time is coming soon enough! If a few tears are shed (by either of you) during the process of getting out the door, there is always tomorrow.

Before you head off to work, though, take just a minute to look that precious baby in the eye, give him one huge car seat kiss, and hold onto the feeling of her snuggle for the rest of your day.

PART 2: WORK SIDE LOGISTICS OF MATERNITY LEAVE AND RETURN

WORK SIDE LOGISTICS:
DEVELOPING A MATERNITY LEAVE PLAN

Want to make a good impression on your manager and employer as you prepare to go out on maternity leave? Jewelyn Cosgrove, a brilliant mama and alumna of the Mindful

Return E-Course, explained to me why a maternity leave plan is a great idea for a mama-to-be and how to craft one your employer will love.

HERE ARE JEWELYN COSGROVE'S THOUGHTS ON CREATING A MATERNITY LEAVE PLAN

I'm a career-driven momma-to-be. Of course, when you have a career, one of the biggest stressors you encounter as you prepare for a new baby is planning your leave. I know experiences vary widely depending on where you work and the nature of the job, but hopefully sharing my plan with you will help you consider how best to develop yours.

By taking the Mindful Return course, I focused a lot on handling mommyhood. But at the back of my mind, I was concerned with how to manage my career along with my new role. We've all heard the horror stories about how going on maternity leave can impact pay and advancement; I desperately didn't want to lose out. As I listened to other mothers, I came to the conclusion that keeping my employer's needs in mind before I left could make my leave more restful and less stressful. I wouldn't be worried about my work, I knew my employer wouldn't resent me because we had planned together how to manage my assignments, and it would be clear I take my work obligations seriously. A well-done maternity plan can achieve all of these things.

I crafted my own maternity leave plan for my employer. I tried to be thorough and opted for a more formal approach to lay out my priorities in a way that also kept my company's priorities in mind. Your maternity leave has a significant impact on your supervisor, co-workers, and direct reports. The more you can prepare them for your departure, the more you remind them of their value, and the more seamless your transition will be because everyone is prepared.

A comprehensive maternity plan needs to keep three things in mind: (1) your responsibilities at the office, (2) how you want your leave to be handled, and (3) how you want your transition back to work to be managed. These areas are all important for you to think about in advance so you can help your employer plan for your absence in a way that makes you comfortable. Most importantly, it lays out expectations for your leave on both sides of the career equation, giving you the space you need to adapt to your new life and your employer the chance to manage your absence in a way that meets their needs.

Here's how I tackled my own plan:

1. **Before going on leave.** I provided my employer with a list of projects I would complete in advance of my departure. I front-loaded these projects so that for the most part, I could complete the vast majority before the baby arrived. I also provided a list of my ongoing tasks that would need coverage in my absence. I have no direct reports, but if you do, you might take the liberty of recommend-

ing coverage of your duties to specific workers. If you're like me and don't have a direct report, just be sure your plan provides a complete list of your responsibilities so nothing is missed; then you can let supervisors handle the details.

2. **Maternity leave itself.** Next, I focused on my actual leave. It was important to me to plan precisely when I would check back in to get an update on projects before actually coming back. I stated in my plan that I would check in after week 10 (I plan to take 12 weeks) of leave to begin my preparation for getting back to work and that I would not be available for any work-related correspondence in advance of that date. Laying out a plan for when you will check in manages not only expectations for your employer, but also gives you a target to come out of your mommy-daze. For me, it provided a timeline to focus on my new baby and know when I would get back to my career.

3. **Returning from leave.** Finally, I made my pitch for my return, both in the transition back to work, as well as long-term. My office allows for teleworking, so I utilized existing policy to request that my transition back into work include a few days of telework to reacquaint myself and catch up on projects with fewer potential interruptions. I also requested ongoing telework accommodations so my husband (who also teleworks a few days a week) and I could manage day care drop-offs and pick-ups without also timing those with a long commute. Ultimately, if

you have the inclination to have flexible hours, tele-working, or a compressed schedule, you actually have to ask for it! Most work places are beginning to think more creatively about satisfying the needs of good employees who just happen to be parents; don't miss out on a chance to provide value even through this huge life change.

Throughout my plan, I kept my employer's needs in mind. I didn't over-ask, and I addressed obligations directly throughout. When I presented it, I was open to discussing the details—particularly around coverage of my responsibilities and any adjustments to the schedule that may be necessary.

Much to my surprise, my employer LOVED my plan. My boss immediately signed off and my HR director raved about how holistic the approach was. I credit the fact I made my leave turnkey for them for easy acceptance. I knew my office culture and had a pretty good sense of what I could ask for without going overboard. Showing my respect for the corporate culture, utilizing existing policies to their maximum benefit for myself, and making sure they knew they—as an employer—were being respected and considered within my plan . . . well, it worked to my advantage!

WORK SIDE LOGISTICS: A FEW NOTES ON THE ACTUAL WEEK OF RETURN

Common—and effective—strategies for returning to work after maternity leave include starting on a day other than

Monday (so you have a shorter week to grapple with) and phasing back into full days. These great tips on timing don't necessarily assuage a new mama's worries about not being able to catch up on everything she missed while she was out on leave, though. When I came back from leave, I couldn't help but think to myself, "How will I possibly have time to do the work that's required now *and* read my email backlog, learn what happened while I was gone, and feel like I don't have a big knowledge gap?"

With my first kiddo, my reentry mindset was entirely unhelpful. I tried to catch up on everything I missed while I was out, plow through all those emails . . . and quickly got overwhelmed.

My advice? Schedule 30- to 60-minute meetings with your key stakeholders at work (direct reports, bosses, key members of your teams) throughout the first few weeks you are back. Ask them to give you highlights of what happened while you were gone and advise you on how you can contribute best *right now.*

Then, let go of whatever happened. Do not read every old email. Do not worry about knowing every detail of what happened while you were out. Instead, look ahead and focus on what you can add to the team moving forward.

Also, before you go back, get in touch with other working parents at your office or who work near you and set up lunches with them for the first week back. They will be able to relate to what you've been through for sure. If you shed a few tears over lunch, they will not judge you, and chances are, you will look forward to lunch with some good adult (though likely kid-related!) conversation.

WORK SIDE LOGISTICS: BATTLING DISTRACTION (A.K.A. GETTING THAT FOCUS BACK)

As a new mama, does your mind ever jump from place to place and to-do after to-do? If so, you are definitely not alone. Both at work and at home, I tend to have a million and one things on my to-do list, and if I'm not careful and intentional about how I spend my time, I tend to hop from one thing to the next. Feeling like I never have a solid stretch of time to work on one thing makes it hard to get *deep* into those projects that require more than just a few minutes of effort.

Though I'm a big fan and advocate of being fully present at work when you're at work, and being fully present at home when you're at home, that's so hard to do when it seems like a million unfinished things are hanging out there.

One technique I learned that I simply love is the so-called "Pomodoro Technique." Named after the Italian tomato (and a tomato-shaped kitchen timer), the idea is to commit to working in a focused way on *one* project for 25 minutes, with five-minute breaks between each 25-minute session. If your mind starts wandering or if you think of other things that need to get done while you're in the middle of that 25 minutes, you simply write them down and go back to the task at hand.

I've never been so efficient and productive—or gotten such a charge out of being focused—as I have when I've used this technique for getting things done at work.

Home, of course, can be a different story. I don't know about you, but in the life of a new working mama, snagging a solid chunk of 25 minutes (awake!) may as well be like sneaking away to the spa for an afternoon. Impossible. So at home, I lower the timer to a more realistic interval for this stage in life. My husband and I like to tackle clutter in the evenings with the timer set for 10 minutes. And I use Insight Timer in five-minute intervals to fit in micro-self-care.

Try out just one or two "pomodoros" (as the plural form of that 25-minute increment is called), and see if you get that same sense of focus and psychic boost.

Then, at the end of the day, let it all go. Let whatever you did today be enough. Parenting IS distracting, mama. No two ways about it.

WORK SIDE LOGISTICS:
WHEN LAST NIGHT WAS A DISASTER

My kids are a bit older now, but I still remember vividly those nights of being up five or more times. Maybe it was a growth spurt, perhaps a sleep regression, maybe baby was getting sick... it was sometimes impossible to tell why the chaos was happening. I remember when the longest consecutive stretch of sleep I got was about 90 minutes. I was truly a mess and all I could do in the morning was cry. I was a wreck and wondered (without answers) how to pull myself together to get to work in the morning.

Until I discovered this secret (yes, a secret . . . perhaps don't advertise this at work): if you possibly can, drop off baby at day care or with your caretaker, tell the folks at work you will be in by lunch time, head home, and *go back to sleep.*

I know this is not always possible—whether you have a meeting you cannot miss, or a plane to catch, or a job that requires your physical presence. Sometimes, though, it *is* possible, and when it is, you should *use* the flexibility you have to get your head in a better place. Think hard about whether your presence is truly required; and think hard about what will serve you, your employer, and your family better. Heading to work a complete mess—or—getting an hour or two of sleep so you can put yourself back together?

Have I done this? Yes, you bet. I did not abuse the flexibility and probably did the go-back-home-to-sleep thing three or four times during the first year of each of my kids' lives. It made the world of difference. Sometimes, you just cannot function and something has to give.

Forgive yourself mama. No guilt. And go back to bed. Mindful Return's orders.

WORK SIDE LOGISTICS:
NEGOTIATING WORK FLEXIBILITY

Now, I offer you a dare. A dare to ask for something in the workplace that will help make this new life you have created a tiny bit easier to navigate. I'm asking you—just for a moment—to toss aside all the assumptions you have made about what you are "permitted" to ask for, and how people will respond. Because you really don't know what the answer will be until you try.

There are countless ways to incorporate some level of flexibility, remote work, and phasing back into work after maternity leave into your life. I know not all of these are options for everyone, and some of you have more rigid schedules than others, but with the rise of telework, flexibility is expanding. If some form of flexible schedule is possible for you, I dare you to breathe and grow into a schedule that works both for your employer and for you.

When I was pregnant with my first child, I had a boss who literally said of my maternity leave, "Take what you need. Email me what you want your phase-back-in schedule to look like." My first thought was utter thrill at the generous possibility of crafting my return. Then, however, I felt terror at not knowing what was "acceptable" to ask for.

I wound up asking for and taking 20 weeks of maternity leave (at the time, my employer offered only one week of paid parental leave, but I had sick and vacation time for the rest). I also phased back into work for the first month by working slightly longer days each week. The first week back, I worked from 10 am to 3 pm, and I worked from home Thursday and Friday. The short days definitely helped me work out the kinks with day care drop-off and pick-up logistics and allowed me to adjust to being away from my baby. The second week back, I worked 9:30 am to 4 pm, and worked from home on Friday. And so on.

Two things I retained from that first maternity leave were working from home on Fridays and leaving work at 4:30 pm every day (no matter what!) to go pick up my kids from day care before it closed. At my previous job, I had this arrangement for over four years, and it worked for me and for my employer. One reason it worked, however, is that I was—and continue to be—flexible with my flexibility. At one point, for example, I was leading a team for a few months that could only meet on Fridays. So, I stopped my work-from-home-on-Fridays plan for about six weeks to accommodate the needs of the team, and I picked it back up again as soon as we were able to move the team meetings to other days of the week. When I have the occasional evening work commitment, my husband and I work out an arrangement (when my kids were smaller, this usually involved having one of our day care teachers come over to help with bed and bath time so we had two adult sets of hands in the house!) so that I can go.

I have since left the employer where I worked when I went on maternity leave with both children, and I am now a partner at a law firm on a 60% schedule. I negotiated this arrangement as part of my offer (given that I wanted to devote the other 40% of my time to Mindful Return and to my kiddos), and I am happy to report that it has been working out well. In general, I work for the firm Monday through Thursday, with a hard stop at 4:30 pm to get my kiddos, and I don't work for the firm on Fridays. Again, I'm flexible with my flexibility though—I will log on after the kids' bedtime if necessary, and if a client needs something on a Friday, of course I help out. And then, I make it up to myself another day.

How do you pop the question of asking for some flexibility? This varies by employer and by supervisor, of course, but try these steps, whether you are still pregnant, out on leave, or already back at work:

1. **Dare to dream.** Sit down with a pen and paper and brainstorm all the things you *could* ask for.

2. **Do your homework to inform this dreaming phase.** Talk to other working parents at your place of employment to

see what their arrangements are. (If you're in a billable hour world, find out what part-time options *really* mean.) You may be surprised at what flexibility your colleagues have been able to negotiate for themselves. If the results of this environmental scan are not encouraging, don't write off your own ask anyway. Everyone's supervisor is different and there is a first time for every arrangement.

3. **Decide what you will ask for.** Commit to making the ask.

4. **Find a good, quiet time to have a conversation with your supervisor.** "Hey, can I talk to you for a minute?" while she is darting off to lunch probably won't be the most effective way to make your case. Schedule some time on her calendar.

5. **Start the conversation by focusing on your and your supervisor's shared commitments in the workplace.** You are much more likely to engage your supervisor and her interests if you commit to quality, punctual work in addition to a balance that will help you live your work and family lives well. For example, ask questions like, "How can I best help the team move forward as I transition back?" and, "How can I best help *you* with your current priorities during the transition?" All illustrate your commitment.

6. **Be calm. Be peaceful. Be flexible.** You may not get a yes the first time. Consider this conversation as the beginning of an ongoing dialog with your supervisor about your life-with-family work schedule, not an all-or-nothing, once-

and-done talk. In this vein, consider asking for flexibility on a trial basis (perhaps for three to six months), to be re-evaluated after a few months. Your supervisor might be willing to commit to something temporary as a trial run.

Why dare to ask? Your sanity and your family's. You can't know what you might get unless you ask.

WORK SIDE LOGISTICS: LOGGING BACK ON AT NIGHT (A.K.A. THE "SPLIT SHIFT")

How do working parents manage to get in a full day of work if they leave at 4:30 pm to pick up their kiddos? The answer for many of us is in the so-called "split shift." The concept is that a parent ends the workday "early" to spend time with children and finishes up that workday after dinner, bath, and bedtime. In other words, you're still working a full day, but you've time shifted a bit.

"How on earth does anyone have the energy for this? I've been asked by brand-new mamas. "How can anyone possibly have the motivation to log back on without being resentful, frustrated, or downright too tired?"

I *absolutely* use this strategy to get things done (there is no other way to be a partner at a law firm and run a company while wanting to be there for my kiddos). Here are my four secrets to how I've managed to make the split shift work for me:

1. **I did NOT do the log-back-on thing at the very beginning.** For the first six-plus months that I was back at

work (okay, make that closer to a year), I was simply too (insanely) exhausted even to think about logging back on after I managed to get the baby to sleep. Neither of my kiddos slept particularly well the first year of their life, and neither did their mama. Nevermind that while pumping there was all that pump-part cleaning and bottle prep work to do in the evenings. Back in those days, I collapsed into bed at ridiculously early hours of the night and resigned myself to doing whatever I could for work during my workday. It simply HAD TO be enough. And it was.

2. **I use my "break" in the day to recharge me.** Now that my kids are older (three and five), I don't mind the logging back on at night. I actually find that the 4:30 to 9 pm device-free break from work I take each day to pick up my kids and BE with them and my husband recharges me and gives me new ideas and a second wind. I love playing in the backyard with my boys for a bit after school, catching up with my husband over dinner, helping my oldest with his Lego sets, and reading and singing as a family before putting the kids sleep.

3. **I split my split shift.** Part of why the evening working works for me is that I use a fair chunk of it for Mindful Return—which is truly a passion of mine and does not feel like work. I prioritize any pressing client legal work that *needs* to get done, and then I turn to Mindful Return to use a completely different skill set and side of my brain. I also triage work and try to reserve deep thinking and heavy writing for daylight hours when my brain tends to be sharper.

4. **I give myself a hard stop.** Depending on how much (or how little) sleep I got the night before, how I'm feeling, etc., I pick a time that I'm going to stop working and head to bed, and I stick to it. It is not always the same time every night, but choosing a time leads me to check in with my body and determine what I should and should not work on that evening.

I know the split shift is not for everyone, and too much can lead to being overwhelmed by work. But for now, this approach to work is working for me.

WORK SIDE LOGISTICS: THE BLUES—AND BLISS—OF WORK TRAVEL AFTER BABY

When I took my very first work trip away from home, my first son was six months old. I did a whirlwind 36-hour trip from Washington, DC, to Chicago to give a talk at a conference, and I was undeniably a disaster. My heart and body physically ached at leaving him longer than an eight-hour workday. I remember staring longingly at any airplane-bound baby . . . sobbing uncontrollably in the airport bathroom . . . and pumping while sitting in my airplane seat. (Yes, that was incredibly awkward, but I could not figure out where else to do it, and I was leaking.)

At that point, my son wasn't interested in taking a bottle from anyone but his day care teachers, so I wasn't even sure he would eat while I was away. And while everyone told me "at least you'll sleep the night!" that simply was not true; I needed to interrupt my sleep at some crazy hour to pump. When my talk was over, I literally ran to a taxi, feeling that sense of "must be with my heartthrob NOW" urgency one feels in the first few months of falling in love.

My little trip was just that—little. But it felt like a huge deal at the time. I could not even fathom how some of my friends with little babies had gone away longer—for days or weeks— and further—some traveling internationally with coolers of dry ice to bring home their pumped milk. When I went away on longer trips, I was lucky enough to be able to bring my little guy with me (my husband has a flexible schedule so could watch him during my conferences). While bringing the baby has its own set of challenges, they do not include missing him desperately or pumping gallons of milk.

Things change as our kiddos grow, of course. Now that I'm past the hormonal issues associated with giving birth and breastfeeding and have been sleep-deprived for roughly five years, I have a very different perspective on work travel. Now I *can* sleep the night in a gloriously comfortable hotel bed. Now I *can* enjoy a nice, long, meeting-free, mommy-request-free airplane ride. Now I *can* leave my children cards and notes and do video calls with them in a meaningful way. Now they wave and blow kisses to me as I get into a taxi to head to the airport, and while I still miss them, I do take time to revel in a night of cocktails with colleagues followed by eight hours of uninterrupted sleep.

If you are planning to take a business trip without baby after your return to work, here is what I recommend:

1. **Focus on the good things.** If your baby is tiny, the best thing about your trip may be that your baby gets to bond with someone else. And that someone else may get to learn a few things about caring for baby and holding down the fort that they did not previously know. (These are things you can and should continue to expect of them even after you get home!)

2. **Breathe in deeply the change of scenery.** Been sitting in your house with baby for a few months while on leave? Tired of the stacks of paper in your office? Focus on the work trip as a way to awaken your senses to something new. Consciously breathe in some new and different air and sights.

3. **Sneak in some self-care.** On work travel, I've managed to sneak in everything from a pedicure, to a walk on the beach, to a nap, to a yoga class, to some shopping, to a Broadway show. I also like to bring my journal with me; nearly all my journal entries since having children have been written from airports.

4. **Be present to your feelings.** No use fighting them. Just feel. Take them in. And keep moving through them. One day at the airport, I found myself wanting to scoop up a little toddler stranger and kiss him, which told me yes, I miss my boys. It is okay to acknowledge the missing. Then, when that feeling has passed, it is okay to feel good about taking time for yourself and your career.

5. **Know that baby will be FINE. Just fine.** On that first trip I took, it turns out my son did not drink anything for about 12+ hours. And then he caved, of course, and guzzled a few bottles of milk when he got desperate. You've inevitably left the baby with a competent caregiver—so trust that all will be well.

On the flip side, if you are thinking about bringing your baby with you on the trip and you can swing it . . . my advice is to go for it *now*! Before she can run and raise hell on an airplane; or before he reaches an age where routine is absolutely king; or before you have a second kid, when the whole prospect of traveling with them will make you crave a blissfully quiet trip alone.

WORK SIDE LOGISTICS: TO BUY OR NOT TO BUY? WHAT'S A NEW MAMA BETWEEN SIZES TO DO ABOUT WORK CLOTHES?

It is easy to get confused about your new mama wardrobe, especially as you get ready to head back to work. Not being a fashion guru myself, I reached out to Lani Inlander, personal stylist at Real Life Style, to help answer that tricky question: to buy or not to buy? Here are her great fashion insights.

HERE ARE LANI INLANDER'S THOUGHTS ON POST-MATERNITY WORK CLOTHES

One of the most frequent fashion conundrums I'm asked about is whether or not to buy new clothes during transition times such as after pregnancy or when you've gained a few pounds from stress. It is natural to think you would be wasting money by purchasing new clothes when you think you will fit back into your "regular" clothes within a few months. This is simply not true. You are actually wasting time not feeling good about yourself when you DON'T buy yourself some new clothes. Lest you think I'm being extravagant, I have a simple strategy for you!

Here are my five tips for shopping while in between sizes:

1. **Keep it cheap and cheerful.** Shop at stores like H&M, Old Navy, and The Gap, where you can get the most fashion for your money.

2. **Go for the trends.** If you aren't spending much you can reasonably assume the clothes won't last very long. So why not embrace the trends this season?

3. **Buy what you love.** If your post-baby belly is making you blue, cheer yourself up with a bright top or scarf. Yes, you should get a basic black and white tee, but you should also get a hot pink striped one

if that is going to keep you excited to get dressed each morning.

4. **Make it flexible.** Boxier tops will still look good with skinny jeans when you are skinnier, a cotton maxi skirt will shrink with you, and a scarf always fits!

5. **Invest in accessories.** Wearing good shoes, a pricier bag, and an expensive pair of earrings will up the perceived value of any outfit. And best of all, they'll always fit!

How about a black maxi skirt instead of the fallback yoga pant for new moms and others not wanting to deal with denim? A scarf and relaxed silhouette of a top distract from a larger top half and a long black skirt can shrink the lower half. Add a chic but comfortable leather sandal.

A blazer smooths any lumps around the middle and dresses up a t-shirt. Look for fun earrings that brighten up the face and give you a natural glow. Joggers are another great alternative to yoga pants, but they're still appropriate for running errands or picking up the kids. A tailored, pointy flat keeps the look structured and chic.

WORK SIDE LOGISTICS: NOURISHING YOUR BABY WHEN YOU ARE PUMPING

I could write an entire book just on pumping at work—there is so much to say, and this one little section of a chapter just will not suffice, I know. There is now an entire book specifically on this subject. Check out *Work. Pump. Repeat: A New Mom's Survival Guide to Breastfeeding and Going Back to Work* by Jessica Shortall.

For now, I will share a few things that worked for me during my approximately 20 months of pumping on the job.

I breastfed both of my boys until each was 13 months old, and I felt like a slightly-insane milk machine both times. Every day, I lugged a huge bag full of pump parts to work, and every night, I spent what seemed like hours washing them with bottle brushes, sterilizing them in microwavable sterilization bags, and re-packing for the next day. I also had the added fun of having excess lipase in my milk, which made it turn sour after four hours if I didn't scald it at 160° for 15 seconds. So, I also had what looked like a science experiment going on under my desk after each pumping session. The entire experience was exhausting, logistically challenging, and maddening at times. Yet it was also extremely rewarding, nourishing for my babies, and helped me feel an important connection to them throughout the day. Ultimately, I wouldn't have done it any differently.

Here are a few lessons based on my experience:

1. **The pump.** Those advice-givers are not kidding when they say you need a serious double pump for work. I will not get into a discussion of brands here, but there are some that just get the job done better and faster than others. Read the reviews. And if someone offers you their old pump, well . . . let's just say I got two used ones gifted to me by

mama friends and my kids turned out just fine. I kept one pump at home and another at work (nice for avoiding lugging the heavy pump itself home every night), and I had enough sets of pump parts to avoid washing them after each pumping session. I have also heard from lactation consultants that it is fine to refrigerate pump parts between pumping sessions to save time. (Since I have pumped, the "Freemie" has also arrived on the scene—see the next section for a description of how this fantastic invention works.)

2. **Space.** I know I was incredibly lucky to have had my own private office at work, where I simply stuck a "do not disturb" sign up, closed the door, and went to town. Yes, I had the awkward walk from my office to the communal fridge with some canisters of what was obviously breast milk, but otherwise I really was not inconvenienced on the space front. For you mamas who do not have this luxury, know that under the Affordable Care Act, your employer (if it is of a certain size) is *required* to provide you with a suitable, clean, private place to pump. Yes, I know this means potentially coordinating schedules with other colleagues who may be pumping, and a huge inconvenience to have to get up from your desk and build this into your day. I truly feel for you. Know that you do have the right to request and receive this space.

3. **Timing.** If you do have control over a pumping space and some control over your schedule, it pays to schedule pumping times into your day—even before you return

from maternity leave. I learned from my first return to work that blocking half-hour times on my online work calendar and marking them as "hold" for several months out was a good trick for being sure to carve out time during the day to pump, and assuring that others would not schedule me into meetings during that time. I knew I had to work around standing meetings on certain days, so I planned in advance to try and block roughly—if not exactly—the same time for pumping each day.

With my first baby, I pumped three times per day—once around 9:30 or 10am, another time around 12:30 or 1 pm, and a third time around 3:30 pm. For one reason or another, I had a much more ample milk supply with my second child, allowing me to pump only twice a day—around 10 am and 2:30 pm. (This was, incidentally, a good lesson that all children are different, so do not assume that your nursing or pumping experience will be the same if you decide to do it again.)

4. **Getting a let-down.** For those of you new to this pumping game, this means actually getting the milk to come gushing out as it does when your baby is drinking whole-heartedly. With my first baby, I really needed to relax and look at a photo of him or watch a few-minute video clip of him to get a let-down. With my second baby, I think I was so conditioned to pumping at work, that I actually couldn't get a let-down unless I started multi-tasking— holding the pump in place with one hand while responding to emails with the other. Writing that makes it sound

awful and cold, but hey—you go with what works here. There are bras that hold the pump into place so you can have both hands free while you pump, but those just never seemed to fit me right.

5. **Quantity.** A constant stressor. Am I producing enough? Why does the quantity vary so much day-to-day? One day I might have pumped 16 ounces and the next only 10 ounces... why? The uncertainty had a tendency to drive the control freak in me more than a little crazy. With my first baby especially—with whom my milk supply was lower—I was always worried about how much I was producing. This in turn caused me to get stressed, which lowered my supply. A vicious cycle.

All I can say here, mamas, is pump what you can. Relax and enjoy the ride as much as possible. Know that your supply will wax and wane. Breastfeed with your baby as much as you can on weekends to keep your supply up. If you are still on leave now, pump or hand express some extra—especially first thing in the morning when your supply tends to be higher—to freeze for those days when not as much comes out. With my second baby, I would nurse him on one side in the mornings and hand express the other side into a bottle while he drank. I never had to work for a let-down that way! Ultimately, however much milk you are able to make is an amazing gift to your baby.

6. **Bonus tip on quantity and milk storage.** One of my early quandaries when pumping was how many ounces to store in one a specially-made breast milk freezer bag, knowing

that I did not want to waste a single ounce. My solution? As I was freezing milk in the evenings after work, I intentionally froze it in a wide variety of different ounce increments, so I could mix and match. At any given moment in my freezer, you could find bags with any number of ounces—from one ounce to six ounces. I discovered that if I put any more than six ounces in one a breast milk storage bag, I wound up losing milk to a bag explosion.

My biggest piece of advice on milk quantity is to let go of the live-or-die-by-every-ounce mindset. Pump what you pump, wherever you are able to pump it. Supplement what you supplement, and know that however you nourish your baby, you are doing enough, mama.

7. **Pumping and work travel.** This could be the subject of yet another book, I'm afraid. I pumped on planes, trains, and automobiles, in the Halls of Congress, in the bathroom at government hearings, and in hotel offices. No matter which way you look at it, it's a pain.

   Tips: (1) be sure to have fresh batteries for your pump's battery pack on hand so you can pump from anywhere (low batteries do make it harder to get enough suction to get milk out); (2) call ahead to wherever you're going to see if they can find a pumping room for you and a refrigerator; and (3) see if your employer will pay for a service like Milk Stork (more on this service below), which allows you to send milk home daily in a refrigerated box so you don't have to lug the milk around with you. Even you don't call ahead, don't be shy about asking hotel staff where the industrial refrigerators are if you're at a conference in a hotel where you're not spending the night. And if you are spending the night, don't let the hotel charge you for that fridge in your room. Just say, "I'm breastfeeding!" really loudly in the hotel lobby and they'll take that charge right off your bill!

8. **Nourish YOURSELF to nourish your baby.** Keep a stash of healthy snack food in your office at all times. Prepare to eat a FULL meal for lunch every day. And drink GALLONS of water from sunup to sundown. Pumping is hard physical work and burns TONS of calories. You will definitely produce more milk if you drink water pretty much constantly (I peed more pumping than when I was pregnant...), eat healthy snacks throughout the day, and don't skimp on lunch. My snacks of choice were Greek yogurt and cereal bars in the mornings; another cereal or granola bar in the afternoon; almonds, fruit, muffins, and always a bowl of oatmeal before bed. I also ate a huge, hot lunch every day at work. Simply put: I was constantly starving and feeding myself helped me produce more milk.

Clearly, there are a lot of logistics to work out, but the good news is that with all the practice you get, all this will become second nature in no time. You CAN do this, mama. And remember: NO GUILT about any of it. No guilt that it takes time out of your day. No guilt when you spill some milk. No guilt if you give it up entirely. Do what you can on the pumping front and move on.

WORK SIDE LOGISTICS: WHAT IS A "FREEMIE?" A GENIUS INVENTION FOR PUMPING MAMAS

My kiddos are now almost four and six, which makes my own pumping days pretty much ancient history. When mothers in the Mindful Return course (MindfulReturn.com/e-course) started talking about the "Freemie," I was intrigued—though admittedly mystified by how this contraption worked.

To enlighten me—and all of us—I invited an alum from the course, Jewelyn Cosgrove (also author of the section above on how to create a maternity leave plan), to give us the real scoop on the Freemie.

HERE ARE JEWELYN COSGROVE'S THOUGHTS ON THE FREEMIE

When I got pregnant, I knew I wanted to try to breast-feed. Emphasis on the word "try." I know some women struggle, and I knew there was a chance I would as well, but I wanted to give it my best.

Once my baby was born and she successfully latched and nursed, I set my sights on a new goal—six weeks. Just six weeks and supposedly things would get easier, so I'd try to make it to that point.

Once I made it to six weeks, I decided three months was my new goal, realizing that any longer than that and I would need to be prepared for the challenges of not just being a working mom, but a working pumping mom.

As my return to work approached, my anxiety rose. I was fortunate that my place of work was incredibly accommodating. They installed blinds on my office window, a lock on my door, and provided a fridge beside my desk: everything I needed for privacy, storage, and discretion. But I was still anxious, realizing that I'd essentially have to disrobe in order to pump, and maybe even mutilate a bra to hold the flanges in place. In my job in particular, I'm not always in my office. Trying to keep my pumping sessions on a schedule—when at least one day a week I would be out of pocket—was a daunting additional hurdle to my nursing/pumping strategy.

That's often the biggest complaint for working moms: how to be discreet, maintain privacy, and handle the rather complex logistics of pumping on the go. It's not always easy.

A week or two before I was to return to the office full-time, another mom in my community mom group shared her latest pumping find—Freemies. "They fit in any bra!" She raved to us. I immediately Googled the product. I was skeptical and a little perturbed that I'd need a "conversion kit" to suit my pump, but I decided to make the purchase.

Mamas, the Freemies have been a lifesaver. They fit into literally any bra, and other than the fact they're hard to fit in your shirt if you wear something with no give in the chest area, I can wear whatever I want and never disrobe to pump. I simply tuck the cups into my bra and plug in the tubing, turn on the pump and let the magic happen. I have pumped in my car, I have pumped on Capitol Hill, I have pumped at the airport, and I have pumped at my desk. Not once have I needed to remove even one article of clothing. A friend of mine even pumped on the beach!

Here's how they work. The Freemies are simply collection cups—with a filter, a valve, and a funnel that fits over your breast just like the original flanges that came with your pump. The cups tuck into your bra, making you look a little like Madonna in that famous cone bra, except these seem infinitely more useful. The conversion tubing fits onto your pump's existing tubing so nothing changes from how you would otherwise operate your pump, except for the part that collects the milk. After you're done pumping, you can pour directly out of the collection cups into your storage bottles or bags. Pretty simple, right?

If you're a working nursing mom and have any concerns about your privacy, the discretion and comfort afforded by the Freemie collection cups may be a great fit for you. I know it's hard, but I'm sitting here nine months into my breastfeeding journey and I am really pleased I made the decision to buy the Freemies. Sure, it's an additional expense on top of all the other accessories you may have purchased to compliment your pumping journey, but it's one I've found immensely valuable.

WORK SIDE LOGISTICS: IS MILK STORK WORTH IT FOR SHIPPING MILK HOME WHILE YOU TRAVEL?

Another invention that arrived after my pumping days is the we'll-ship-milk-home-for-you-while-you-travel services. Not having tested these myself, I asked Liz Lapetina, a new mama and graduate of the Mindful Return E-Course, to share her observations on her firsthand experience with Milk Stork, the company that touts itself as "the first and only breast milk delivery service for business-traveling moms like you, providing no-fuss, refrigerated, express shipping of your milk to your baby back home." How does it work, exactly? Is it worth the cost? Here is what Liz had to say about her experience using Milk Stork.

HERE ARE LIZ LAPETINA'S THOUGHTS ON MILK STORK

I've been a management consultant for eight years, so I consider myself a travel pro. I can fit clothes for a week of work travel into a carry-on bag. I have arrived at the airport for a flight that departs 15 minutes later—and made the flight.

I headed back to my consulting job when my daughter was five months old, and my biggest concern was how she would do with our nanny. My second biggest concern was how I would be able to continue traveling light while still pumping. For my first work trip, I packed the bare minimum clothing, wore a single pair of heels the whole trip, and managed to cram my pumping equipment and two mini-coolers into my carry-on bag.

My second trip was more complicated: I was facilitating a two-day meeting in Miami, so there was no way I could get away with wearing the same suit two days in a row! My return trip home involved a tight 45-minute connection, making me leery of checking a bag. So, I investigated my options, found Milk Stork, and decided to use them for a trial.

The Milk Stork model is simple—you order the service for each trip by filling out an online form indicating where you will be staying during your travel and where you want your milk shipped. Milk Stork ships a package to your hotel or other destination. Inside the package is a small box with a user-activated cooling unit and six NUK-brand milk storage bags.

When you are ready to ship your milk home, you activate the cooling unit, pack the box with up to 34 ounces of milk, seal the box with stickers, and then leave the box at your hotel for a FedEx pick up. Your milk arrives chilled at your home the next day.

Being a sleep-deprived new mom, I initially booked Milk Stork for the wrong dates, giving me an early reason to test their customer service. There is no phone number on their website; all communication is via email or FaceBook Messenger. I had a few nervous hours waiting to see whether they could ship a box to my hotel in time (I was arriving two days after I booked the service). They came through, confirmed that they could change the dates, and had a box arrive at the hotel the day of my check-in.

Milk Stork's website and package instructions encourage you to watch a video to learn how to activate the unit correctly. I'm not particularly handy or technical, but I found the instructions for activating the unit to be very clear and easy to follow—you push a button to activate the cooling unit, place it back in the box, and check after an hour to make sure the unit is cool. Mine only took a few minutes to get cold, indicating that it was working.

My only complaint about the service is the measly amount of milk that fits into each cooler. I assumed I could be clever with packing my bags and squeeze extra milk into the cooler, but they are quite small and their estimate of 34 ounces max is accurate. Each shipment costs me over $100, so given the amount of milk you can ship in one package, the service is expensive. For work trips of two days or less, one cooler was sufficient, but for longer trips, multiple coolers would be needed, pushing the cost even higher.

My verdict? It's expensive, but if you are committed to pumping for your baby and can stomach the cost—or have a supportive employer willing to reimburse the cost of Milk Stork—it's a great option and secure way to ensure your milk arrives home cold and ready for your little one.

BONUS: SOME PUMPING POETRY

To conclude this pumping discussion, I leave you with a short tribute to your efforts that I hope will bring a smile (and remind you a bit of Dr. Seuss).

OH, THE PLACES YOU'LL PUMP!

Congratulations!
Today is your day.
You're off to Great Places!
You're off and away!

You have bottles in your bag,
You have milk in your boobs,
You can steer yourself
Any direction you choose.

You're on your own. And you know what you know.
And YOU are the mama who will decide where to go.
You'll look up and down hallways. Look 'em over with care
About some you will say, "I don't choose to go there."
With your head full of brains and your bag full of ice,
You're too smart to pick a pumping spot that's not nice.

And you may not find any
You'll want to go down.
In that case, you'll want to
Head straight out of town.

But you can't of course
Because that milk is leaking,
And you need a spot quick
Where no one is peeking.

Perhaps you'll find space in a lounge just for you,
Or perhaps in your office you'll know what to do.
But maybe you're out and about across town
In which case you'll need somewhere to set your stuff down.
A bathroom will do with your battery pack;
Just prop up that pump and do not look back.

Some days that milk will just squirt right on out
While your pump goes thump, thump
Making you want to shout.
But some other days you will just sit, sit, sit, sit,
And the milk just won't come. Not one little bit.

So you'll wait, breathe, and squeeze
To get a drop or two, maybe
While staring at pictures of your little baby.
And when you relax and the milk starts to come
You'll feel some relief that your job here is done.
Until next time, of course, in three hours or four
When those breasts will fill up and you'll need to pump
more.

Take heart, my brave pumping friends, wherever you be,
In cars, planes, or trains, where the world can see.
Whether you eke out a single ounce or ninety-nine,
It turns out your baby will turn out just fine.

WORK SIDE LOGISTICS: NOURISHING YOUR BABY WHEN YOU ARE NOT PUMPING

Given that I did have the experience of pumping, I turned to a friend and wonderful mama, Kerry O'Brien—a high school biology teacher and cross-country coach—to write about her experience nourishing her baby while not pumping.

HERE ARE KERRY O'BRIEN'S THOUGHTS ON NOURSHING YOUR BABY

This advice is directed at new mothers, like me, who probably feel very similar to how I felt when my son was born 16 months ago and how I often still feel now. The feeling of not knowing what you are doing, the feeling that you have to do the "right thing" for your child . . . and always second-guessing yourself as to what that "right thing" is. I am here to tell you my story of how I handled breastfeeding, pumping, and switching to formula. My hope is that my story will help you see that the "right thing" is so hard to define and so unique to each mother and child. I hope you are empowered to do what is right for you and your family and feel good about it.

All throughout my pregnancy, I read and was told "breast is best" and, as a scientist (I have a PhD in molecular biology and am a high school biology teacher), I very well understood the benefits of breastfeeding.

As such, I was determined to breastfeed for as long as I could. My goal was six months, as I planned to go back to teaching after that time, and the thought of pumping in between classes at school (I teach at an all-boys school with mostly male faculty, too) was just too much for me to handle logistically. So, six months was my goal . . . the right thing in my mind. Well, I made it to four months. At the time, I beat myself up a good bit about stopping (second-guessing myself), but I really knew it was the best I could do. Now, looking back on it, I wish I hadn't beat myself up as much.

Breastfeeding was a struggle for me from day one. Who knows why, it just was. I'm a biology teacher— this type of stuff is supposed to come naturally to me, right?! But it didn't. Yet, I was determined and kept at it. Then, at three weeks old, my son was di- agnosed with a stomach condition (pyloric stenosis) that required surgery. Our world was thrown upside down. The doctors said it was a routine surgery, but nothing is routine at three weeks of age. Long, long story short, we were in the hospital for five days, which were probably the hardest five days of my life. My son made it through surgery like a champ. I was a mess. My son couldn't eat for over 24 hours during that time period, so I was pumping to preserve the supply. Once he could eat again, he had a hard time regulating his intake, and he spit up a lot. I truly felt like I didn't know how to feed him.

Slowly, we realized that we were all a little more comfortable with bottle-feeding. My son really liked eating from a bottle, and I liked knowing exactly how much he was eating. I did a combination of breastfeeding and pumping/bottle feeding until he was eight weeks old, when we introduced formula (as a mix with breast milk). My baby liked formula. As time passed, my husband helped me realize that I was a happier person when I wasn't worrying about pumping. Yet, I felt like it was selfish of me to think about my happiness! This was about my baby and what was best for him. After many, many, long, long conversations with lots of people—friends, family, doctors, and therapists—I finally saw that my happiness was very key to my son's happiness. If I was happy, I could fully enjoy being with him. As I weaned him off of breast milk, my anxiety levels went down. I was so much happier. We were all happier. When my son was four months old, I stopped pumping and switched him completely to formula. I am still self-conscious about not breastfeeding longer, but I know it was best for us.

Lori asked me to reflect on how to "nourish your baby when you are not pumping" and really, for me, I feel like I finally breathed a sigh of relief. As I said, my baby loved his bottle. He started holding it by himself when he was eight weeks old, and my husband and I cuddled with him while he drank. I also feel like I nourish my baby in so many ways when he is not eating. I sit on the floor and play with him; I read to him; I sing songs to him; I chase him around; I show him how much I love him and that he is 100% worthy of my time.

When I started back to work after six months, I didn't have to worry about pumping. I did worry about how I would maintain my bond with my baby. All that "nourishing" I did . . . .how would I maintain it? My solution was to spend the time before and after day care fully dedicated to him. I'd pick him up at 5 pm from day care and play with him, hold him, etc. until it was bedtime at 7 pm. I'd take time to read a book to him before I left him at day care in the morning. My hope is that these thoughtful actions on my part show my baby how much I love him.

As with most things in the land of parenting, this is a work in progress. As a very Type A person who loves to plan and have plans, I have come to a place of accepting that life simply can't be fully planned out when you have a child. The one day that I have to be at work early, of course my son would have a diaper blowout on the way to school. The day of my biology final exam, he came down with a fever. I wish I could say that I just rolled with each of these punches. I didn't. I am slowly learning and realizing that it will all get done and it will all work out, just maybe not the way I planned or the way that I once thought was the "right" way.

As you make your transition back to work, my advice is to be kind to yourself. Whatever it is you need or feel is best for your child, do it. It will carry over to your child. Try not to second-guess yourself. Know that it will not be a linear path. Each day is an adventure.

WORK SIDE LOGISTICS: NAVIGATING SELF-EMPLOYED MATERNITY LEAVE

Being your own boss and navigating maternity leave comes with its own challenges. Not having been self-employed during my own maternity leaves, I decided to turn to someone who has been there, done that. Arianna Taboada, a maternal health consultant, was self-employed on her recent maternity leave and has some fantastic advice to share.

HERE ARE ARIANNA TABOADA'S THOUGHTS ON NAVIGATING MATERNITY LEAVE AND SELF-EMPLOYMENT

Maternity leave can be a complex issue to navigate. As Lori's work so poignantly addresses, many of us face the challenge of a significant socio-cultural silence about what it means—career-wise—to design a maternity leave plan that honors those precious weeks and months of transitioning into motherhood while balancing our professional identity and growth.

For many, factors such as national and state protections (or lack thereof), workplace policies, culture, and personal finances all weigh heavily on your decision. For the self-employed pregnant woman like me, some of these factors matter and some don't.

Let me tell you, negotiating maternity leave and return to work can be flat-out confusing when you don't have a set structure or workplace expectations. Learning what others did and do was invaluable to me. I'm sharing my experience in hopes of shedding light on the unique challenges faced and how I tackled them. I hope my fellow self-employed folks find this helpful.

A little bit about me and my work: I am a public health social worker and make my living as a maternal health research consultant. I also have a small private practice where I offer one-on-one postpartum planning services. Although I live in Mexico, much of my work is with U.S.-based projects and clients.

To be perfectly honest, I had no idea what my options were for leave. So, being a researcher and all, I began by analyzing the variables at play.

What did I know about my business model and related factors?

1. As a self-employed person who lives in Mexico, I do not qualify for the paid leave policies here. All time taken would be unpaid.

2. I contribute 50% of my household income; so I would need to account for this by either saving, billing ahead of time, or asking my husband to pull in some extra work. (Fun fact: he is also self-employed.)

3. My research contracts typically are for three to five years of services, so although I am not an employee, I would need to negotiate how long I could take off with the projects that have an active contract.

4. My private practice varies month-to-month, so this could easily be put on pause and started up again at my discretion. I also have some very strong professional convictions about leave that came into play as I planned my leave.

What did I know about best practices for postpartum care?

1. There is strong empirical evidence of long-term physiological and psychological problems being associated with inadequate rest and recuperation after childbirth. The longer I could take, the better, scientifically speaking.

2. There is also strong research evidence that motherhood takes time to transition into and needs plenty of support. Going at it alone or with limited people to support you is the least expensive option, but it can have costly outcomes down the road. I would need to invest in support.

3. I am trained to be a kick-ass advocate and negotiator about maternal health issues at the research and policy level; however, I feared I wouldn't be able to use this skill set effectively when it came to my personal experience. I needed to advocate for myself!

I started with my absolutely ideal scenario:

- Slow down my private practice workload during pregnancy.

- Start official leave at 38 weeks.

- Be completely unavailable (no client calls, emails, or meetings) for 12 weeks postpartum.

- Begin to be available (minimal hours) via email only at 13 weeks postpartum (equivalent to 15 weeks of official leave).

- Work my way up gradually back to my regular hours over the course of a month. Resume regular work hours at 20 weeks postpartum.

This would mean I had transition time on the front end and the back end, which was the most important thing to me: time to ease into motherhood and develop my "working mama" identity instead of throwing myself into it with no time to process.

I pitched the plan to my three biggest clients, and they accepted it without any additional negotiating! Having a concrete plan and evidence about why this plan was best for both us made for a strong pitch. I also presented details about how ongoing duties would be covered and took responsibility for hiring and training graduate students and internal staff to competently cover some of the things for which I would otherwise be the go-to person.

Another truth bomb: I am sure not everything will go as planned. The Type A professional in me cringes at the thought of my plan going awry. But the compassionate advocate in me says it's OK.

I am learning through every step of the process. Learning to navigate the inevitable unknowns of pregnancy and motherhood is part of the journey.

WORK SIDE LOGISTICS: RETURNING TO WORK A BETTER MANAGER

For those of you who manage others as part of your role, it's important to think strategically about how to manage your direct reports as you leave and return. For some great advice on this topic, I reached out to Stephanie Weeks, a brilliant mama and an alumna of the Mindful Return E-Course, who is Head of Design at Amazon Business. When she took her maternity leave and wrote these reflections, she was the Vice President of User Experience at a company called Blackboard.

HERE ARE STEPHANIE WEEKS' THOUGHTS ON HOW MOTHERHOOD CAN MAKE YOU A BETTER MANAGER

The advice I find most often (though still not nearly enough!) about returning to work is about managing your personal experiences and managing the expectations of your supervisor. That is extremely helpful, but what about returning to work when you are the supervisor? What's different? What's needed? What can you expect?

As an executive in my organization, I have the wonderful opportunity to lead a department of highly skilled and experienced creative staff. They direct themselves and work as a cohesive team. While I was on my 16-week maternity leave, one person on my team really took the opportunity to provide leadership to the group.

He was resourceful and thoughtful, making sure to only include me as much as I wanted to be included while I was out. In these ways, I had the best-case scenario to be returning to work. Even with this, I learned three important lessons immediately upon reentry:

1. Jump into Culture

I have built great relationships with the people on my team so I knew I would be missed, generally speaking, but I didn't realize how my absence would really impact them. One person complimented the person who filled in for me but also said she thought the team felt the missing presence of their leader. She said, "You create the culture here, and we missed that."

As leaders, we do create culture. Intentional or not, your team looks to you to know what the appropriate behavior is, from what to expense on a work trip to how to negotiate difficult conversations to how to distinguish good versus great. More than 80% of employees report that "their relationship with their direct supervisor has a big impact on how happy they are with their job." (CBS, 2013)

What can you do about it? Be there when you return. Really be there.

- Set aside scheduled time on your calendar to catch up with everyone on your team—not just your direct reports. Spend time drafting communications about what you are doing to dive back into things and follow that with regular updates.

- Find something to celebrate! A lot happens while you are out, so it should be easy to find.

2. Listen Carefully; Act Quickly

The reason I was able to glean these insights around culture was because I was listening. Challenges are bound to happen while you are out on leave and the one-on-one conversations I had with team members revealed them. By listening carefully to multiple people, I was able to quickly spot trends—misfires as well as successes. Trends are something you can act on quickly. I was able to hear their stories, diagnose, and create an action plan. More than one person told me how thankful she was for being able to talk with me directly (especially if she did not report to me directly), and for seeing action happen so quickly after my return.

How to do it? Completing the steps below within the first two weeks of your return will set you on a strong path toward reentry with a happy team:

- Send out correspondence immediately upon your return that you are glad to be back and will be diving in immediately to know where you can best be of service to the team.

- Set up time with a representative sample of your team (or all of them if you can!), and ask two simple questions: "What's working?" and "What's not working?" Put your own ideas on hold until after you talk with people.

- Make an action plan with your management staff based on your findings, and designate at least one small thing that you can do immediately to make an improvement.

- Send out communication to the team about what you learned and what you and your management team are going to do about it.

3. Relate Better with Your New Mama Skills

One of the things I learned while taking the Mindful Return Course was that I can use my new skills found in motherhood in all sorts of ways. For me, compassion is the greatest thing I can contribute at work.

As a manager and a parent, I now have a much clearer understanding of what it means to have important, non-negotiable pulls on you outside of work. I've been open about my new understanding of this to my team when it has become relevant.

I have had two employee-initiated discussions about working hard while being a parent in just my first month of returning to work. Both employees were touched, and I think our working relationship has only improved. I became a more "real" person to them and they felt more understood by me.

Companies are made up families, not just employees. I have the ability and strength to make my professional contributions because of the love and support of my own family. Likewise, as employers, when we get great contributions from our team, we can recognize their support network enables them and appreciate the full picture.

Finally, a word on being a mama and a company leader. Statistically, women's careers stagnate at least temporarily when they have a child. This frightens many professionally-driven women—it certainly frightened me. There are so many choices at this point in our lives. If one of those choices includes being a leader in an organization, I challenge you to talk openly about being a mama. Too often, there is a sense that you should go on maternity leave but then return to work just the way you were before; in other words, to not be a mama while you are at work. If you are a mama, be one at work; don't hide it. The women in your company need to hear it and they need to see you succeeding. Even when you show up without makeup and with spit-up on your suit, stand tall. You are doing this! The women in your company have someone to look to if they choose a similar path, and the men can feel confident in their decision to follow such a strong and real leader.

PART 3: CRITICAL SKILLS FOR *BOTH* WORK AND HOME

SKILLS FOR BOTH WORK AND HOME: DRAWING BOUNDARIES

Five years into this motherhood adventure, I have discovered that one of the *most* important skills to learn for improved sanity has been figuring out what on earth to do about boundaries—that is, how to (1) define, (2) set, and (3) honor them. Boundaries are, after all, one of those concepts in life that is quite simple (draw a line!) . . . but really, really hard to implement.

I will walk through these three steps to living with effective boundaries, one at a time:

1. Defining "Boundaries"

Look up "boundary" in the dictionary, and you'll find "a line that marks the limits of an area; a dividing line." I really love the analogy to a playground with a fence, though:

> *"Boundaries are a source of liberation. This truth is demonstrated elegantly by the story of school located next to a busy road. At first the children played only on a small swath of the playground, close to the building where the grownups could keep their eyes on them. But then someone constructed a fence around the playground. Now the children were able to play anywhere and everywhere on the playground. Their freedom, in effect, more than doubled."* — Greg McKeown, Essentialism

A boundary keeps what you want in your life at a particular moment, in. It keeps what you don't want at that particular moment, out. Fences have gates and doors, and you can choose when to open them and walk through.

2. Setting Boundaries

To "set" a boundary, you need to decide what you want to live on either side of it—which often requires a good bit of thinking, journaling, noodling, doodling, and brainstorming.

As I returned to work after maternity leave, I had to think hard about what I wanted my work schedule to look like, which included things like setting end-of-day, work-from-home, and remote-availability boundaries. I ultimately landed on a hard-stop-go-get-kids boundary of 4:30 p.m. (as my day care closed at 5:45 p.m., and I needed to get there before 5:30 p.m.), work-from-home Fridays, and evening-post-bedtime online availability (the so-called split shift, discussed on page 102). To keep what I want "in"—i.e. quality time with my family during dinner, bath, and bedtime—I set a tech-free boundary around my 5–9 pm window.

Sometimes you can decide in isolation on the boundary you want to have, but more often, boundary-setting requires a negotiation with other humans who also have opinions about their own boundaries. If you want flexibility at work, you'll likely need to negotiate it with your supervisor and your team. If you want to set a boundary at home, your partner and your children are probably important constituents in the equation. For example, as I've mentioned, my husband and I both committed to a weekly meeting to consolidate chaos in our home—we then had to set a boundary around the time of day and day of week to hold this meeting.

Boundaries can be set around time, of course, but they can also be set around feelings, interactions, actions, and commitments. I *am* willing to sit with and feel deeply a sadness I am experiencing about my baby (admittedly, not-so-baby anymore) getting so big I can hardly carry him. I am *not* willing to spend time with someone in my life who leaves me feeling depleted. I am *not* willing to engage with my toddler during this tantrum. I *am* committing to five minutes of meditation tonight.

3. Honoring Boundaries

Okay, so now you have a good idea of what a boundary is and what boundaries you would like to set. I think the most important thing about boundaries isn't setting them but honoring them. It is easy enough for me to *say* I will stop work at 4:30 pm or put my phone down from 5 to 9 pm, but it is another thing entirely to do what I have just committed to. The key to honoring boundaries in a way that makes them work (for your sanity!) is sticking to them more often than not, and to walking through that fence door when it makes sense to do so.

To stick to a boundary, perhaps the most critical skill I've learned is saying no (which I discuss in more detail in the next section called "A Thoughtful Formula for Saying No"). Brené Brown, the famous shame researcher, also has a perspective on boundaries that is simply awesome:

> *"I also practice setting and holding boundaries. Saying no is hard when you're trying to please everyone, but it's way easier than feeling resentful. My boundary mantra is,* **'Choose discomfort over resentment.'** *If you are coming toward me with a PTO sign-up sheet and you see me quickly close my eyes and start chanting—you'll know exactly what I'm saying."*

To honor a boundary—and honor yourself—it needs to be okay (and not another source of guilt) for the boundary to be permeable at times. When the General Counsel of a hospital client of mine calls my cell phone at 5:30 pm and says she has the Hospital CEO on the line, I don't tell her to call back later. When a friend makes a surprise visit from out of town on a weekend my family had reserved to do nothing, I see my friend. When we are invited to a dinner party on a Saturday night, we move our Saturday meeting. And when a kiddo is home sick on my work-from-home-get-yoga-in-first day, I skip yoga. Of course.

You *can* do the work to set and honor good boundaries, mama. Here's to brainstorming what boundaries you need, allowing them to be permeable when they need to be, and believing in their power to liberate.

SKILLS FOR BOTH WORK AND HOME:
A THOUGHTFUL FORMULA FOR SAYING NO

I'm definitely the type of person whose natural reaction to a (reasonable!) request is an enthusiastic "yes!" I love being able to contribute when people ask for my input. I like to be an engaged colleague and friend. I like the work I do, and I want to give back to my friends and family. Quite honestly, I find it flattering when someone calls and asks if I'll take on a leadership role with an association related to my field.

But I know I simply cannot say yes to everything—every option, every request, every opportunity that comes my way—if I want to focus on what's important to me and take good care of myself in the process. Since having two kids, running a business, and working full-time, I have simply had to become better at prioritizing; curating my days, weeks, and months; and pointing a laser focus on the "need to dos" rather than the "would like to dos."

That kind of prioritizing requires a good deal of turning others down, though, and I have discovered over time that there are certainly better and worse ways to say no. There is a "no" that can burn bridges ("I'm too busy, leave me alone!"), but there is also a "no" that can actually improve your relationships and boost your professional profile and reputation.

Here is the formula I like to use to decline a request in a professional, respectful way:

1. **Express enthusiasm for what the requestor is trying to accomplish.** For example, "The association you're asking me to take a leadership role in has been really important for my professional development, and I really couldn't be more grateful for what it has given me professionally."

2. **Explain your current circumstances.** For example, "As you might imagine, having just started a new job a few months ago with two little kiddos under five and a business to run, I'm a bit pressed for time these days."

3. **Express openness to revisiting the request in the future.** For example, "Please, please keep me on your list and reach out to me next year if you find you have the same need."

4. **Offer to help find others who might be able to help.** For example, "I'm happy to help you brainstorm names of other people you might ask or who might be able to help. Email me about this, and I'll send you the names of some of the colleagues I think you should reach out to."

Yes, this all takes slightly more time and effort than either ignoring the request or responding with a grumpy "forgettaboutit." But, if your goal is to be known as a collaborator, team player, and contributor in your community, the extra effort is worth the few additional moments it takes to be professional and respectful. Your personal brand will thank you for opting for the thoughtful approach.

SKILLS FOR BOTH WORK AND HOME:
STORYTELLING AS A MAGIC POTION

"Tell me a story, mommy," my five-year-old said at bedtime last night. "But make it be about aliens who live on the biggest, longest planet ever, and all they eat is dessert," he instructed. "Got it? Ready, set, go!" After asking him a few clarifying questions (Any particular kind of dessert? Did the aliens have teeth or had they rotted out from all the desserts?), I thought for a moment and got rolling with the age-old "Once upon a time . . . "

I have been thinking a lot more about storytelling these days, now that my boys can and do ask for stories with frequency. They want imaginary stories of Vikings and leprechauns living in a volcano in South Carolina, to be sure, but they also want to hear stories about my own life and theirs. Like the time I jumped off a moving train in Siberia, went to Chicago for work and bought them toy airplanes, or went to the hospital to give birth to them. And, being children, they want to hear the same stories again, and again, and again. Heaven forbid a detail change from one telling to the next!

Looking back, though, my storytelling didn't begin when

my kids were old enough to ask for stories. Oh, no. It started when they were in utero, when we'd describe to the baby what kind of (wacky) family he was going to be born into, or how mommy was feeling really ready for baby to come out. And when each baby was born, I found myself telling them stories of my day—my metro commute, which hospitals I was helping at work (I am a health care lawyer), and what I had for lunch.

As you transition into and travel down the road of working parenthood, try these storytelling strategies to help weave together your own past, daily present, and imagined future:

1. **With your babies.** Tell them where you are headed when you leave in the morning, and tell them stories about your day when you get back. Also, expose them to your workplace at an early age so they can visualize where the story you are telling is taking place. When my babies were tiny, I took them each to my office to meet my colleagues. I have fun photos of them lying on a changing mat on the floor next to what looks like a monster-sized desk compared to their little peanut bodies. I incorporated these photos into their baby book, and they know the stories of how they came to see mommy's work friends when they were babies. I continue to take them to my office from time to time so they can see where I work . . . and can play on my computer and draw on my white board!

   When your children get older, you can start a dinnertime tradition of asking each family member to complete the sentence "the best thing that happened to me today was . . .", giving everyone a chance to tell a story and be heard. My boys love doing this—so much so that they fight over who gets to tell his story first.

2. **With your partner.** I first learned about the positive psychology principle of "capitalization" from a clinical psychologist friend. The underlying premise is this: if you don't tell someone else about your own good news, you're leaving on the table much of the benefit you could have gotten from that good news. On your way home from work, can you think about something good that happened to you that day? And can you tell your partner a story about that thing when you get home?

3. **Stories you tell yourself.** Consciously and unconsciously, we're telling ourselves stories all day long. Are the stories you tell yourself *helping* you weave together your work and home lives into a seamless and striking tapestry . . . or are they tearing you apart into shreds of guilt and anxiety?

When I went on work travel, I used to tell myself the story that I was abandoning my children and shirking my responsibilities as a wife and mother. Not helpful, right? Retelling that story as one about a woman who is strong enough to (1) step aside to let someone else grow that special bond with baby (while refining parenting skills!), (2) set an example that women do travel for work, and (3) use the travel opportunity as a time to recharge and clear her head, has changed entirely my own mindset about travel. What story are you telling yourself around child care? That it's not natural for someone else to be caring for your baby, or the historical truth that so-called "alloparents" have been helping in the care of children for all of human history? (Thank you, Brigid Schulte, for this revelation.)

One final piece of advice. If the thought of telling a story on demand gives you hives, take a deep breath and know you *can't* tell a wrong story. If you live and breathe and think and talk and write, you already tell stories every day. And if you find yourself saying, "I'm not a good storyteller," perhaps it's time to rethink that story you're telling yourself about what kind of storyteller *you* are. Your stories are *yours*, mama, and your family members will love them because they represent *you*.

Oral stories have existed as long as humans have been able to communicate. They are how we learn, grow, and get to know ourselves and one another. If we start telling them to our little ones from birth—indeed before birth—they just may help us feel like our work and home lives are a bit more interwoven.

While I may not have thought it was anything special, my son loved the toothless dessert-eating alien story I told last night. "It was good, but just not *long* enough!" he exclaimed, before snoring a moment later.

TURNING LEAVE INTO LEADERSHIP

"To be authentic is literally to be your own author (the words derive from the Greek root), to discover your own native energies and desires, and then to find your own way of acting on them. When you have done that, you are not existing simply in order to live up to an image posited by the culture or by some authority or by family tradition. When you write your own life, you have played the game that was natural for you to play." — Warren Bennis, *On Becoming a Leader*

CAN LEAVE LEAD TO LEADERSHIP?

Welcome to our chapter on exploring leadership in the space of returning to work after your maternity leave.

Why am I including lessons on leadership here? Two reasons: (1) I had the good fortune to learn from a truly inspiring leadership coach, Amy Jacobsohn, who worked with me before, during, and after my second maternity leave. She gave me tools that empowered me to think in new ways about going on leave and about the opportunity I had to be a leader upon my return. I would like to introduce you to my coach, and share a conversation with her.

And (2) I truly believe that *all* moms, no matter their industry, skill set, or title, can be leaders in the workplace who can help make the working world a more hospitable place for working parents. I know there are lots of places where working moms still do not have a voice or are not well represented, and I hope our work throughout this chapter will inspire you to find—and use—your mama leadership voice.

I am most grateful to Amy for agreeing to allow me to interview her here.

HERE ARE AMY JACOBSOHN'S THOUGHTS ON WHAT IT MEANS TO BE A LEADER

Lori: Amy, before I started working with you, I didn't particularly think of myself as a leader, but you changed my mind and helped me realize that truly anyone can lead. What does being a leader mean to you?

Amy: For me, a leader is one who carves out a new way forward. It's that simple.

In the most lofty sense, I like to think of leaders as those who wake us up, remind us what matters most, and guide us toward the realization of our dreams. Leaders shine a light beyond the well-trodden path and point the way to a new future we never before thought possible.

Lori: Do you believe leaders are born or created?

Amy: Created. We are all leaders in many aspects of our lives. Leadership is not dictated by age, title, or appointment. You can lead one person or millions, on any topic or any challenge. Leadership isn't luck or happenstance. It's a deliberate act of courage; a willingness to stand up against the rush of the tide, and say, "I see another way and it shall be."

Great leaders are inspired by something beyond ego, something bigger than personal benefit. Their vision becomes their rally call or North Star, and it shepherds them forward. To suggest that a leader is "born that way" not only makes us victims of the hand we were dealt, but disregards what it took for the leaders who came before us.

Lori: Can you give us some examples of what leadership might look like for a new mom in the space of going on maternity leave and then returning to work?

Amy: Moms returning to work after maternity leave return to a wide variety of titles and roles. Yet no matter what their "level" or scope or work, all have an opportunity to provide meaningful leadership.

The question isn't so much which opportunities for leadership exist for new mothers, but rather where each woman wishes to apply her leadership.

There is no right answer. It's just a matter of what's most meaningful to any given woman, and the possibilities are endless.

Is it changing the way you feel about *yourself* as you return to work after maternity leave, i.e. self-leadership?

Is it connecting new mothers and sharing tools and tips to support them in their transition as you, Lori, are doing with Mindful Return?

Or maybe it's nothing specific to being a new mother at all, but rather you wish to bring all your new insight and learnings and perspective to a work challenge that is meaningful to your career aspirations.

Lori: You and I spent a lot of time on self-leadership. What do you mean by this?

Amy: Well, I don't know about you, but my mind can be a wild and wooly place to visit. I sometimes think of Maurice Sendak's book, *Where the Wild Things Are!* Even the best of us are besieged by a jungle of thoughts and emotions, not all of which are particularly empowering.

From my perspective, self-leadership is about doing the work to transform the jungle of our mind into a hospitable and empowering place, maybe a place you'd even want your children to visit.

Lori: Amy, as you know from working with me, new moms can be really hard on themselves. What would you say to them?

Amy: We women are fascinating. We go to great lengths to protect the people we love from the bullies of the world, and then we bully our own selves relentlessly.

So, the first thing I'd say is to practice self-compassion. We are our own worst enemy. It's time to start leading the way by being our own greatest champion.

LEAVE AND LEADERSHIP: GET CREDIT FOR THIS

Building on Amy's wisdom, let's think about how you can view your maternity leave through an empowered lens or filter and carve out a new way forward for yourself and others. For me, my predictable path forward was that upon my return, I would try to avoid the topic of having been gone. But what would life look like if I didn't avoid it? If I looked at it as something at which I succeeded? Something where I shined?

Today, I offer you the idea that as a leader who adds your valuable voice to the mix at work, you can and should take and get credit for a well-planned and executed leave and return. It is never a bad thing to be known at work as thoughtful, intentional, and well-prepared, and your maternity leave gives you the opportunity to showcase these skills.

If you have not yet gone on leave, I urge you to take the time to prepare your teammates well for your departure. Teach them skills you think they'll need while you are gone. Give them one-pagers on key contacts—what to call them for and how to reach them. Make step-by-step lists of critical tasks.

If you are already on leave, give some thought to how you would like to reintegrate into your projects, teams, and workload. (And, if you are already back, it is never too late to turn over a new leaf, and adopt a fresh perspective.)

Upon returning from my first leave, I was so focused on catching up on what I had missed—and never really being able to—that I constantly felt behind . . . like I had missed too many important things while I was out. The second time around, with some important help from my leadership coach,

I was able to focus my attention on moving forward instead of on that gap of time I was gone. Toward the end of my maternity leave, I scheduled two or three meetings per week for a month or so with various colleagues, asking them two things: (1) to give me a short debrief on key things that had happened while I was out; and (2) how I could best help them moving forward. And then I didn't look back.

Where does getting credit for what you've done to prepare for leave fit into this leadership conversation? With your organization's goal-setting and performance evaluation process. (I know not all organizations require formal goals, but I presume everyone's performance gets evaluated somehow.) If you do have to craft formal goals, and there is still time in the goal-setting cycle, I encourage you to set a professional development goal for yourself around planning your leave and return. And at evaluation time, I urge you to highlight for your supervisor all of the ways you were prepared, thoughtful, and organized about how you passed the baton to your colleagues.

Supervisors can be busy and have a lot on their plates, so it pays to outline the steps you took and remind them about how responsible you were about your time away from your job. I was fortunate to have a supervisor who, on her own, took note of and applauded my leave and reentry efforts in her written and oral evaluations of my work. I also wrote about my planning process in my own self-evaluation to refresh her memory.

Your maternity leave can be an opportunity to remind your colleagues of your best qualities, about why you are a valuable member of the team, and how you can be trusted to handle life events with preparation and poise. Having a well-planned approach to leaving and returning—and taking credit for my planning—helped me feel more confident about my leave. Knowing plans were in place both for leaving and for returning helped me free up emotional energy for my kiddos. None of that could have happened without leadership.

LEAVE AND LEADERSHIP: GROW YOUR TEAM

When I was seven years old, my parents went away for a week and left me and my brand new two-wheel bicycle at my grandmother's house. I had never ridden a bike before—even one with training wheels—and my parents decided it was time for me to plunge in and forget the training wheel idea altogether. I remember being both thrilled and terrified of that beautiful pink Schwinn, and I begged my grandmother to help me ride it.

I feel lucky now to have had a grandma who was fit enough to run alongside my bike on the sidewalk for hours while I was learning and who was also patient enough to stick with me until I got the hang of riding. But after she saw that I could go a few feet my own, she stepped back and watched me from her porch as I wobbled and fell. She told me to brush myself off and keep going. After she saw that I *could* get my balance by myself, she never again laid her hands on those white handlebars.

As you approach your leave, you may have the opportunity to teach colleagues what you do in your day, and train them on skills or subject areas that are new to them. It will probably make everything go more smoothly—and will make your life easier—if you know you are leaving things in capable hands.

My challenge to you is to think about how you will interact with your colleagues upon your return. It may be predictable that you would take back all your old work and continue on as though you had not left. Yet, perhaps there are ways to make your leave a growth experience for everyone.

The first time I went on maternity leave, my boss took over all of my work while I was gone. She had trained me on everything in the first place, so I didn't take on the role of teacher as I headed out for leave. I did, however, chair a sub-committee of my local Bar Association at the time, and in my role had singlehandedly been planning events for local young health lawyers. The way things were going, if I was gone, there would be no events. A colleague urged me to consider using my leave to really solidify and institutionalize the work I had been doing—so I put out a call for interested committee members, got about 10 responses, and with that, the New Practitioners Committee of the DC Bar Health Law Section was born. I continued to co-chair the Committee when I came back, but I am proud to say that I rotated off and it has continued on without me now for years.

For my second maternity leave, I had a direct report who had just started working for me about four months before I was due. She had quite an intense orientation—both to her job and mine—in a short span of time, but she was a quick study. She did an amazing job while I was gone, and I admit to wondering how we would divide responsibilities—how she would continue growing, and I would remain relevant—upon my return. I was honest with her about my desire not to step on her toes when I got back to the office, and we had great conversations about how to make our reporting relationship work for both of us. I asked her what skills she gained and what work she had learned to do that she wanted to keep doing. I was also honest about what I did really want to take back. We are now true partners, and I learned that teaching her things freed me up to expand the scope of my own work.

Perhaps this section about growing your team is not resonating with your circumstances, and you truly do need to resume all of your pre-leave responsibilities upon your return. If this is the case, perhaps think more broadly. Letting go of the handlebars does not have to be solely about your job. Maybe it is at home with a partner or caregiver. Can you teach someone how to prep bottles for the next day? Pack the diaper bag at night? Are there tasks for which you can write out steps, ask for help, and then stand aside?

After the week with my grandma, it wasn't as though I didn't need her in my life anymore; I just didn't need her for bike riding. By teaching and then stepping out of the way as much as possible upon your return to work, you can position yourself and your team in a space of growth, and you can start to lead in new areas.

LEAVE AND LEADERSHIP:
DECIDE WHAT TO OUTSOURCE

What, oh what should you choose to let go of as a working parent? We all hear that delegation is important both to combat becoming overwhelmed and to advancing professionally, but it is not always easy to figure out *what* exactly to delegate.

I often fall into the trap of believing that many tasks require *me* to do them; or it seems they cost too much to outsource. This is an issue I really struggle with—must have order! must have control!—and I have had to learn to think creatively about ways to let go of certain things. Trying to do it all myself was what put me in a puddle of tears on my kitchen floor. And ultimately, inspired me to create Mindful Return.

Today, I challenge you to put all judgments and opinions aside for a minute and just brainstorm all the things you do in a day (sit with a pen and paper, set the timer for five minutes, and make a list!) and options for who might do them instead:

- **Cleaning your home.** If outsourcing on a weekly basis is too expensive (or exhausting), have you considered hiring cleaning help on a monthly or every-other-month basis?

- **Lugging milk home on work travel.** See pages 119-121 on Milk Stork.

- **Baby care.** Are there things you and your partner can divide and conquer? When our babies were little, I was affectionately referred to as "master dresser" and my husband was "master changer." Can you bring in a parents' helper for a few hours on a weekend to help out? Can you get a babysitter for two hours on a weeknight so you can stay late at work one day a week?

- **Tasks at work.** Can you grow your team by training more junior talent, allowing you to move some things off your plate?

- **Taxes and accounting.** Can a professional do this more accurately and efficiently than you can, whether for home finances or for a business you own? Think about the opportunity costs here.

- **Food.** Perhaps a weekly takeout night is in order? Or a few meals a week from a food delivery service? Or a joint effort at meal planning with your partner using an app?

- **All other things under the sun.** Is there an affordable concierge service nearby that you can invest an hour or two with? Have you explored the world of postpartum doulas?

You *do not* have to do it all, mama, and it pays big dividends in sanity and time to figure out who in your family and extended tribe can help you out.

LEAVE AND LEADERSHIP:
FOCUS ON YOUR NEW SKILLS

Whatever we choose to turn our attention to tends to grow and flourish, don't you think? If I turn my attention to cuddling with and reading with my baby, his smiles get bigger, my own heart gets fuller, and our bond grows stronger. If I turn my attention to an important work project, it gets done on time and with skill. If I focus on all the things I *can't* do in a day, my head goes to what Shawn Fink calls "the land of bitter and sour." If I focus on all the things I *am* doing for my family and my career, I feel pretty darn good about the mother and employee I am.

One of my pet peeves about the average workplace mindset is a perception that women somehow automatically give up focus, skills, dedication, and the ability to succeed, simply by having children. All the attention seems to be on what is lost instead of on what is gained by becoming a mother, and we talk ourselves into thinking we have somehow become less of an employee because we took leave, take time out of our day to pump, or have a hard stop at the end of each day to go pick up children.

If it is predictable that our own minds might go down this same path of focusing on these alleged losses, how do we change what otherwise might have been predictable? Today I'd like to urge you to focus on—and to talk openly about—all the new and amazing muscles you are growing by becoming a mother. If you are new on this journey, some of these skills may reveal themselves to you over time.

Here are a few I have seen mamas develop:

- **Patience and adaptability.** As a parent, it seems absolutely nothing happens according to plan. (Or it will for a while, and then abruptly, the plan changes.)

- **Creative problem solving.** Rarely does the same solution to a baby-related problem work two times in a row.

- **Prioritizing.** When the to-do lists multiply and there simply are not enough hours in the day to get everything done, prioritizing is essential. There are the must-dos, the nice-to-dos, and the time wasters, and having kids helps you get straight really quickly which category each task falls into.

- **Anticipating the needs of your stakeholders.** Little babies certainly are demanding customers, aren't they? And the better you're able to predict in advance what they need, the smoother your day goes. The same is true for your boss' needs.

- **Organizing and planning.** As a working mom, you cannot get out the door in the morning—or get out and actually stay out—without a massive amount of advanced planning. Organization is a survival skill both at home and at work.

- **Increasing delegation skills.** Asking for help on the mama front is critical. As you return to work, it becomes a work survival and success skill, too.

- **Perspective.** Coleen Kivlahan and Tracy Fink talked about this in Chapter 2. Disasters at work just don't seem as bad as they may have been in the past.

Tout your new skills, and remind yourself of them regularly. By putting our focus on those areas where we have become amazing mama ninjas, maybe, just maybe, we can change the conversation about the value of being a working mama *both* in our own heads and in our workplaces.

BONUS: THE RESEARCH SHOWS WORKING MAMAS ARE ACTUALLY *MORE* PRODUCTIVE THAN NON-MAMA PEERS

A recent study from the Federal Reserve Bank of St. Louis featured in *The Washington Post* (Study: Women with More Children are More Productive at Work,*) found that "over the course of a 30-year career, mothers outperformed women without children at almost every stage of the game." Yes, there can be a productivity drop when the kids are little, but guess what? "When that work is smoothed out over the course of a career . . . they are more productive on average than their peers."

This breath of fresh air celebrating working mamas stands in contrast to a *New York Times* opinion piece by Yael Chatav Schonbrun, "A Mother's Ambitions,"** which I admit made me sad. While I give Schonbrun credit for putting her voice out there in a big way,—and for being honest about her feelings of not having enough time to do everything she wants to in her career as a part-time researcher at Brown and a private-practice psychologist—I am worried she does a disservice to effective, intelligent professionals who happen to have children by portraying working mothers as bad employees.

In the article, she focuses heavily on her diminished "productivity" within each of her roles, and declares that she "hated knowing that my mentors and colleagues were not terribly impressed with me anymore." Does she really *know* this or is it her own interpretation of things? She also concludes that "there is absolutely no chance that I will be promoted to associate professor, and I will continue to be an unknown in my research community."

I do not work in academia, so I cannot comment on the path to associate professorship. But, to the comment that she will remain unknown in her research community, I have to ask: doesn't she have some control over how well known she is? Aren't there small but powerful and effective things she could do, with strategic focus, to get herself known? To her

** Opinionator.blogs.nytimes.com/2014/07/30/a-mothers-ambitions/?_php=true&_type=blogs&_php=true&_type=blogs&action =click&pgtype=Homepage&version=Moth-Visible&module=inside-nyt-region&region=inside-nyt-region&WT.nav=inside-nyt-region&_r=2&work)

comment that "my patients get frustrated with my limited availability," I also found myself asking whether that might be a sign she is extremely good at what she does and is in high demand. Won't clients always want more time and availability from the professionals they hire?

I am extremely sympathetic to the idea that working moms simply do not have enough time in the day. I know I certainly don't. The to-do lists we impose on ourselves, whether or not we have children, are endless. I also agree that what Brigid Schulte refers to in her book *Overwhelmed* as the "ideal worker" culture, valuing face time and round-the-clock availability over efficiency and effectiveness, pervades many workplaces and is a force to be reckoned with.

I will speak for myself, however, in declaring that I am a *more* talented employee and leader because I am a parent. I am infinitely more efficient than I was before having children. I set priorities like nobody's business. I have a stronger power of connection now with anyone who has children or ever was one (um, that would be everyone). I have honed my skills on how to anticipate needs. I am more patient. I am better at delegating. I deal much better than I used to with the unexpected. And, taking time to be in the moment with my kids after work every day and play in a serious way with them lets my brain recharge and increases my creativity. Think of the CEO Schulte talks about in her book, the one who takes afternoon walks on the beach to get his best ideas . . . it's the same concept.

Schulte also wrote about a man whose first book took him a year to write. After changing the way he worked—to short bursts of concentrated effort—he was able to write his next two books in under six months each. He worked smarter, not more hours.

Working moms need to be more vocal about the skills we have gained and stop doubting how effective we can be, even with less time on our hands. Yes, there's less time for nonsense, but there is no less time to be thoughtful, mindful, and strategic about what we choose to do and how we choose to use our time. Let's shout from the rooftops that our value as colleagues, employees, and leaders goes *up* when we have babies and come back to work.

LEAVE AND LEADERSHIP: SET AN EXAMPLE

In *Overwhelmed*, Brigid Schulte begins her chapter entitled "When Work Works" with the following two fabulous quotes:

> *"What if I hadn't worked so hard? What if . . . I actually used . . . my position to be a role model for balance? Had I done so intentionally, who's to say that, besides having more time with my family, I wouldn't also have been even more focused at work? More creative? More productive? It took inoperable late stage brain cancer to get me to examine things from this angle."* — Eugene O'Kelly, former CEO, KPMG

> *"While working on* The Last Supper, *Leonardo da Vinci regularly took off from painting for several hours at a time and seemed to be daydreaming aimlessly. Urged by his patron, the prior of Santa Maria delle Grazie,*

to work more continuously, da Vinci is reported to have replied, immodestly but accurately, 'The greatest geniuses sometimes accomplished more when they work less.' " — Tony Schwartz, *Be Excellent at Anything*

As we wrap up this chapter on leadership, I challenge you to think creatively about ways you can change what's predictable in your workplace. Change the dialog. Make things happen that otherwise would not have simply by being there and speaking up.

When my kids were really little, I had a boss who remembers vividly what it was like to be a young working mom with all the unpredictable things that come with having a child. For a few days, one of my boys was home sick, and I was stressed about missing work. When I returned to the office after being out for a few days to care for him, her first—very enthusiastic—welcome was about how my son was doing. She was truly and deeply interested in knowing what had happened and that he was okay. And with that inquiry, WHOOSH, all my dread about having missed work went out the window. She was a leader. She set the tone for my day and my return to the office. And she couldn't have understood so deeply had she not been there herself.

Since becoming a mom, I have discovered new ways *I* can lead in my office, too. In my current job, I'm a law firm partner on a 60% schedule. I am very open and public about not being full-time, *and* about being a committed member of the team.

In my last job, I sat on my organization's retirement plan committee as an "employee" representative (i.e. not from human resources (HR) or finance), and the committee had an important decision to make about whether employees would continue to get their retirement match while they were out on paid leave. No one else on the committee seemed to understand how relevant this was to women who took maternity leave; it was up to me to make the argument that a paid vacation or sick day that a woman had saved intentionally for her maternity leave should be worth no less the day after she had a baby than the day before the baby was born. I certainly didn't know when I joined this committee that I would be bringing my mama voice to the table, but I was honored to ensure that perspective got heard.

Here are some questions to get you thinking:

- Can you set an example of a healthy maternity leave for others at your organization by defining and communicating boundaries about what work you are willing to do and discuss while you are out on leave?

- Can you say to a direct report on a sick day: "Don't worry about work today. Take care of yourself (or your child). We've got this?"

- Are there opportunities to raise the profile within your organization of issues women face when they go on maternity leave and return? (See the next section, How to Form a Working Moms' Posse at Your Office.)

- Whether you manage people now or will in the future, can you relate to them—and help empower their leave—in ways non-parents simply can't?

- Can you use a position of authority you have now or in the future to enter the dialog on what it means to be a working mom, or change policies and attitudes toward leave, return, and balance?

- Are there committees at your workplace that would benefit from hearing the perspective of working moms? Can you join one of those committees? (After you are getting a bit more sleep, of course.)

There are countless ways you can help change the current, predictable dialog and mindset at your workplace. The conversations aren't always easy, and of course it can take time for tides to turn. I know you have leadership in your bones though, mama. You can make a difference just by being there and having a voice. A sleep-deprived, sometimes emotional voice, yes, but one that is also passionate, authentic, thoughtful, and honest. You have been there through the chaos, the ups and downs, the hard work, the love, and the tears. Standing tall and taking action from that beautiful place *can* make things happen.

LEAVE AND LEADERSHIP: HOW TO FORM A WORKING MOMS' POSSE AT YOUR OFFICE

Not long ago, I had the opportunity to interview Rachel Thomas, the President of Lean In and an awesome executive, entrepreneur, and mom of two. She provided some fantastic insights that really resonated with me on how to make the transition from working woman to working mother—all based on her own experiences. One of my favorite pieces of her advice is to "form a working moms posse" by asking other women in your office who have kids out to lunch and setting up a regular rotation to share your experiences.

We all know how important it is not to get isolated and to form a supportive community for ourselves, especially early in parenthood. But how do you actually do this when you are so short on time and sleep-deprived?

Here is how I did it.

When I went back to work from two maternity leaves, I worked at a pretty large association where plenty of women had previously gone out on and returned from maternity leave. So, I thought there would have been plenty of support around the topic. Boy was I wrong. No one seemed to be talking about the leave and return experience, and the conversations I did have were one-off moments of shared desperation that took place behind closed doors.

I knew I could learn so much from my experienced mother-colleagues and thought my workplace would benefit from a parents' group, but with two little kids who weren't sleeping and a full-time job, I didn't feel like I had the time or energy to start one myself. So I hemmed and hawed a bit and grew more and more frustrated with the lack of coordinated support. Finally, I said, "If not me, who?" And decided to do something about the problem.

The most important thing I would like to convey here is that starting a working parents' or working mothers' group at your office does not have to require a huge amount of time and effort, and it can have big rewards for you and your colleagues.

Once I decided to go for it and start a "Returning to Work Community" for new parents at my office, here is the formula I followed:

1. **Brainstorm your target audience and write a short plan of what you would like to do.** Take a few minutes to write out your vision for the group, then put together a short plan (a few paragraphs will do) to lay out what the group might look like. My target audience was new parents—moms and dads—who were planning to go out on and return from parental leave.

2. **Sit down with your human resources department to ask for their blessing, and see if you can get formal support from the organization.** I first talked to the head of my division to make sure she was on board and would support me with human resources, and then I sat down with the human resources manager who was responsible for parental benefits. My human resources department was not only supportive but thrilled with the idea and helped me to advertise the group to anyone who came forward with an announcement that they were expecting a baby.

3. **Get the word out.** Human resources asked me to create a one-page flier to put in their Family and Medical Leave Act (FMLA) packets, and I wrote a short article for our internal employee newsletter about the group. Be sure to

talk it up to your own friends within the company, because they are likely to be your most ardent supporters.

4. **Find a time for the group to meet in person.** We did a once-a-month brown bag lunch in a conference room at the office. I maintained the list of folks who were interested and sent out an online calendar appointment for our meetings. It turned out that only women came to the lunches (a subject for another discussion), and it became a group that mainly consisted of moms with kids ages five and under.

5. **Consider a virtual component.** It was important to me that the group be able to connect between our in-person lunches, so I set up an online community for us. People used it to discuss pumping room issues and workplace policies, post photos of their kiddos, and offer up free baby stuff to colleagues. From time to time, HR would even ask me to use this forum to take the pulse of the group on an HR-related issue.

6. **Consider including "experienced" parents.** Every third meeting or so, we invited folks who had volunteered to mentor us to come and share their experiences with the group. We learned so much from working moms who had been around the block a few times already.

I know you have no extra bandwidth at the moment, mama. When you do have a little, though—and all you need is a little—I'd urge you to take Rachel's advice and consider making this investment in yourself and your workplace community. You will be a happier, more connected mama and employee, with a mentor group you may not have considered, and you will change the lives of other new mamas in your workplace.

LEAVE AND LEADERSHIP: WAYS TO HELP IF YOU ARE MOTIVATED TO CHANGE WORKPLACE CULTURE (ONE BABY STEP AT A TIME)

The new mamas I work with through Mindful Return (www.mindfulreturn.com/e-course) often get fired up about changing workplace culture and making the working world more hospitable to new parents when they go back to the office. All those struggles they have heard about are no longer just theoretical, and they feel a fresh spark that pushes them to make a difference.

The problem is, of course, that new working mamas are exhausted. All brain cells are being used to keep the wheels turning with work, baby, and home, and life doesn't seem to leave much time for concerted action, even around issues they care about.

The good news is that simply *being* a new parent in the workplace gives you the opportunity to be an important model to other new parent colleagues. Others will want to see *that* you are doing it and *how*. To this end, one simple way you can help move the needle is by sharing your own story in a public and beautiful way, by contributing to the It's Working Project's *Portrait Project.* This is "the first comprehensive look at the back-to-work experience in our country, told in the first person, through the lens of those who live it."

- How to contribute? Fill out their online "interview form." I did it, and it took only about 20 minutes. (See, I told you: a baby step!)
- They published my own working mama portrait. Check it out at www.ItsWorkingProject.com/user-story/lori-m.

I love how the "It's Working Project" is painting a candid portrait of new parents in the workplace. If you are *really* on fire and want to do more than share your story or start a parents' group at your office, here are a few more:

- Start a petition on Change.org (a partner of the It's Working Project) to change the picture.
- Follow the work of The Better Life Lab, the think tank led by Brigid Schulte at New America that focuses on redesigning work and gender equity, by subscribing to their biweekly newsletter at NewAmerica.org/better-life-lab.
- Get involved with the ThirdPath Institute, an organization dedicated to promoting an integrated approach to work and life, at ThirdPath.org.
- Follow the work of Valerie Young, a big advocate for family-friendly policies and paid leave at Mom-Mentum.org/blog/category/woman-in-washington.
- Donate to First Shift Justice Project, a non-profit that works to empower low-income pregnant women and parents to safeguard the health and economic security of their families by asserting their workplace rights.

The more of us who are out there taking baby steps, the faster that workplace culture needle will move.

Chapter 5

BUILDING YOUR COMMUNITY

Welcome to the fourth piece of this working mama sanity puzzle: building community. This chapter is, for me, the crux and heart of the matter. Here, we focus on the importance of creating and being in community, even when it's hard to do that. It's so hard because you may have no energy for it, no time, or no desire. I put so much emphasis on this subject, because it was truly community that saved me from the deep, dark place I was in when I went back to work after my second baby.

I could cite you any number of scientific studies about the perils of isolation. Inmates go crazy in solitary confinement. Baby monkeys who can cuddle with even a stuffed monkey are healthier than those with no one to connect with. "It's a very short path to depression and burnout if you lose your sense of mission and connection to colleagues," said the President of the Association of American Medical Colleges, Dr. Darrell Kirch, in a keynote address about physician well-being.

But rather than citing studies (I am no scientist anyway), I will tell you about the intense isolation I felt so deeply when I had each of my babies *and* when I went back to work both times after leave. I pride myself on being fiercely independent. I figure things out for myself and love the thrill of making my own discoveries. I am reluctant to ask for help. And you know what? These skills serve me well . . . sometimes. I didn't see a reason to let go of them.

Add to these traits the fact that I did not have the time or energy to make a whole bunch of new mommy friends, especially when I knew I would be leaving them to go back to work soon. My best friends from college were scattered around the country, and only some of them had kids anyway. I had both of my babies in the winter, so I was not particularly motivated to go out in the cold. Joining certain support groups cost more money than I wanted to spend, and talking about family issues with work colleagues felt taboo. In short, my head was full of reasons not to connect. Not to reach out. Not to turn to my existing communities for support or create new ones.

Until I just. Couldn't. Take. It. Any. More.

And paraphrasing Mary Oliver's beautiful poem *The Journey*, one day I finally knew what I had to do, and began, though the voices around me kept shouting their bad advice. And I left those voices behind and started walking in a new direction. One where I *chose* to take an e-course called the Abundant Mama Project and connect with women from all over the globe about this crazy thing called parenthood. Where I *chose* to sit in my office with colleagues who were also new mothers and *be* with them as they talked through the very struggles I was facing. Where I started blogging and connecting to other new working mamas.

If there is one thing I have become passionate about through my blog and creating the Mindful Return E-Course, it is the critical importance of avoiding that isolation into which we can easily fall. Connecting really saved me from despair. In parenthood, I believe one of the things we need most is resilience—the ability to "climb out of the hole and bounce back." Rosabeth Moss Kantor put it best, when she said resilience "thrives on a sense of community."

Has there been a time—baby-related or not—when you've suffered or are suffering alone? What difference do you think reaching out might have made or might make now? It is worth taking time to remember the perils of isolation so that you can focus on connecting, building community, and being resilient.

BUILDING COMMUNITY

Now we flip the coin and start taking a deep look into the joys of intentionally sharing with others this remarkable experience of being a mama.

First, I share with you the words of my friend, yoga teacher, and founder of lil omm yoga, Pleasance Silicki. I happily fell headfirst into the yoga community she created in my neighborhood when I was pregnant with my second child. When I thought about who best to remind us of the benefits of community, she is the first person who came to mind. You will see that her passion, joy, and love for all mamas shines through in everything she does.

HERE ARE PLEASANCE SILICKI'S THOUGHTS ON THE IMPORTANCE OF COMMUNITY

In the center of a room, a candle glows. A sea of smiles and tears surround us. With tremendous gratitude you hear "OMMMMMMMMM" and then silence. There is nothing more powerful.

Frequently, I am surrounded by the most awake and engaged women in Washington, DC, most often on our yoga mats. As the founder of lil omm yoga, a wellness community, I have the pleasure to work with, know, and celebrate women daily. I started lil omm out of my own desire to connect to other women who wanted to integrate the love and passion for yoga and motherhood. My yoga practice has transformed my life. First, as just physical healing from an injury and then over the years of consistent practice, it has shown me the depth of my own patience, strength, flexibility, passion, and most importantly, LOVE.

I wanted to share this love with others. I wanted there to be a yoga home in DC where women of all stages and shapes and sizes could come join hands and celebrate our commonalities. We are all so similar. At the end of the day, we want to be loved, we want to find work/life balance, we want to be in meaningful relationships and feel supported when times are rough, and the thing about life is, we all will suffer. There will be a time when things are not easy and when we need a connection to something bigger to help pull us through. Welcome to yoga.

Even though I have closed the yoga studio portion of lil omm, the same guiding principles apply to creating community in all areas of my life. I love sharing meaningful content, asking tough, real questions about motherhood and life and being surrounded by amazing thoughtful women along the way.

As moms, we need time to share and connect for grounding and for purpose. When we open up who we are and share with others, we might hear "me, too", or someone might offer a hug, and just that little gesture of being heard is magic. We feel better when we are open and honest with our real lives. We can heal ourselves with our truths. We evolve when we have space to lean into our fears, approach, embrace them, and release them. I see it happen all the time. A strong mama community is painfully honest and unbelievably meaningful to our lives.

Having a community of women to support you during these transitions is of utmost importance for your soul. It's a way to nourish your heart. Over the years, our mom/baby classes were filled with stories of pumping in bathroom stalls or cars, leaking through work shirts, late day care pick up commute nightmares, and various sleep stories. It is so important to have a sacred space that is a non-judgmental, non-exclusive environment just to be heard!

To learn from others in the same boat or to be told: "You are enough. You got this." And, "This too shall pass."

Motherhood can be lonely, can be tough, can be exhausting, and the work we do at lil omm embraces these truths while trying to help us see that all is constantly changing. That each day IS a gift with our babies. That each moment is precious just as it is. That these children we love so dearly ARE NOT our only identity and that somewhere along the way, we will emerge. We are here. Without trying or pushing or forcing or grasping, they will grow.

I did not set out with a business plan to grow community. I just make every decision about lil omm from the heart. I decide whether or not the offerings are going to engage, inspire, and connect people, and I move forward from there. The community at lil omm was created out of my own need to be with others in an intentional way. We respect each other, we speak openly, we say yes, we show up, we breathe, and we stretch. Sometimes by ourselves; sometimes with our families. Lil omm is a place that honors our most intimate relationships as a way to live more peacefully and with more happiness. When you make time for yoga and meditation, for creativity and movement, you see shifts in your life. Things begin to open, to deepen, to get a bit clearer. It's just how the magic works.

When I close my eyes, I see the warmth all around me. I see the rawest form of human beings, the deepest joys, and the darkest sorrows that are all part of our lives. Creating a space where we can be seen, heard, and experience this sense of connection within our fast-paced world saves my life every day.

At the end of the day, I thrive because of this community. I heal because I can work with others and teach, and learn, and study, and give.

My advice to other mamas is . . . .

- Reach out.
- Say YES to life and NO to "should."
- Lend a hand.
- Get out of your head.
- Move into your heart.
- Listen to your intuition.
- Never underestimate the power of community.

Awaken to the fact that for thousands of years, women gathered in groups and shared. We worked side by side. We cared for each other's children. We cried and laughed TOGETHER. It's the most natural thing we can do.

BUILDING YOUR COMMUNITY:
IN-PERSON COMMUNITIES

There is nothing like the sound of an old friend's voice on the phone line, or a hug from your supportive neighbor, the mom with elementary school-aged kids who has been there and done that sleep deprivation thing. There is power in online connection, of course (see below). There is also something so amazingly love-filled and rejuvenating about in-person connections with living, breathing people who make our days easier and help guide us through the good times and bad.

Cultivating this in-person community can, of course, take effort. I know how hard it can be, especially at a time when you don't have much extra energy; when reaching out can seem like being a burden.

I challenge you, however, to explore ways to be sure you are getting the right amount of in-person community-building for you. You will each have a different threshold for the amount of time you need to spend with others who support you, and you won't always "click" with whatever setting or group you join. I urge you to keep trying, though—to find friends and colleagues who resonate with you.

Here are some ways I worked on building my own in-person community during and after my maternity leaves, just to give you ideas to explore:

1. **Known, trusted friends.** I was lucky enough to have two friends who had babies the same time I did, and I relied on them a TON during my first maternity leave. I decided not to join a new moms group (like PACE in the Washington, DC, area), and in retrospect I regret it. At least I had these new mamas I could reach out to at any time of day or night. We challenged one another to get out of the house, went to the nursing lounge at Nordstrom's together, and did a baby feet-painting outing at our local paint-your-own pottery store.

2. **New mama groups and exercise.** I took both pre- and post-natal yoga classes with both of my babies, and loved all the classes I attended. While all of these experiences were great for my health, one was better for my in-person community-building than the others. What made that experience special? For the post-natal class I took, we were required to sign up for all six classes and the same mamas showed up each week. We were all committed to the class, bonded much more, and went out to lunch after each class. The drop-in setting never had that same feel.

3. **Colleagues at work.** I knew there were plenty of women in my workplace who had been on maternity leave and had kids, but no one seemed to be talking about the experience. In an effort to fill this void, I started what I called the "Returning to Work Community" at my former employer. I discovered it was possible, with truly not so much effort, to start a group of new moms who all work at the same place. Wow, did it make a difference in helping us connect and advocate for ourselves!

4. **Nothing wrong with paid community members.** Not having close family in the area—but still wanting to go out on dates—it was important for me to find some trusted babysitters I could rely on. I am incredibly lucky in that the teachers at my kids' day care babysit on the side, and they are now an integral part of the in-person community I rely on so much for support and advice.

Do any of these ideas resonate with you? Can you think of ways you can reach out to and rely on your in-person communities so they can support you in your transition to motherhood and back to work? Let's give one another the encouragement we need to reach out. Your friends and colleagues will be glad you asked for help and connection. I promise.

BUILDING YOUR COMMUNITY:
ONLINE COMMUNITIES

We all know how easy it is to get lost in the online world. To spend countless hours "catching up" on the lives of people who don't mean much to us anymore (or maybe never did). I boycotted Facebook for years and only joined in 2014 to make a page for Mindful Return. I understand the downsides and have plenty of critiques of the online world.

Taking an e-course myself changed my mind about the power of online communities, though. When I signed up for Shawn Fink's Abundant Mama Project, I never realized I would become a believer in the power of social media or in the ability of the internet to help one mama in DC. To connect her with Anglophones from California to Australia to Singapore and not feel so alone in her parenting struggles. The online support networks we create can be every bit as real and as valuable as in-person communities. I strongly believe they should complement—not replace—the real-life interactions we also need to support us, but they are certainly valuable in their own right.

If you are seeking an online community of new working mamas, I invite you to consider joining the Mindful Return community through one of the e-course sessions (www.mind-fulreturn.com/e-course), and staying connected through our vibrant alumnae community. I also urge you to consider the other online communities that might resonate with you. Check out the Abundant Mama Project (www.abundant-mama.com). Explore the city-specific online groups and list-servs in your area. Consider making a private group on social media for other new parents in your office.

To close this section on in-person and online communities, I leave you with a poem I wrote about the experience of taking the Abundant Mama Project e-course.

ABUNDANCE

Eighty wise teachers showed up one morning,
piled out of a tiny clown car and
straight into my sticky-fingered house
with plans to stay the month.

Now fish and visitors stink
after three days,
but these mamas smelled of coffee grounds,
baby shampoo and the cake
my oven had been yearning to bake
for years.

They came from the seaside
and snow (and what snow!),
metros and fields,
big broods and small.
But no matter which

home sweet home where they mopped up
mud, cheerios, and exploding emotions,
they all had big dreams
of candlelight stillness
and the sound of breath
in their own ears and
Big, heavy, delicious love
for their sometimes-sleeping sweeties.

No side-by-side huts,
but I joined their village,
cracked open into cyberspace
and felt a warm, red glow
like ET's fingertip touching mine
each time someone responded to my posts.

And they taught me in short order
to be grateful for the midnight cries and cuddles.
To savor the scratch of the pen in my journal.
That I got this big crazy
thing called parenting.

At least sometimes.
And that I can dance on my doorstep
and sing out loud
that happiness is the truth.

BUILDING YOUR COMMUNITY:
PARTNERS AND PARENTS AND IN-LAWS, OH MY!

As you think about your community, you have likely given some thought to the idea that you will constantly be working with others to care for and raise your children. In this section, we will be pondering how to co-exist within your whole village. Though there are days when it may not feel like it, your partner, child care provider(s), and family *are* all on the same team, wanting your little one to thrive in the world. How you relate to them and interact with them matters.

While they may all be cheering on your cherub, it is virtually impossible for everyone on your team to agree 100% on how to raise your child. Figuring out how you will navigate sharing care responsibilities and those differences of opinion—especially knowing what's important to hold firm to (perhaps a bedtime or naptime routine) versus what's worth letting go of to avoid needless tensions (perhaps a few extra animal crackers)—is hard. Figuring out how to navigate relationships with these members of your team *outside* their care-giving responsibilities (e.g., I'm not having any issues with *you*, just your parenting philosophy on a particular point) is hard, too.

I really believe there are no silver bullets here, but that managing our relationships with partners, parents, in-laws, and other integral members of our communities is a dance of sorts, an ongoing learning curve, and a constant renegotiation. I can offer you no answers, but a few perspectives based on my own experiences.

1. **Partners.** Having a baby really does require a rebalancing of the relationship with your partner. I absolutely felt off-kilter in the relationship with my husband for the first few months (maybe a year?) after my oldest son was born. There were all of the existential questions that hung in the air: "Who am I? Who are we as a couple? Who are we as a unit of three? Who's supposed to be doing what and when?" We didn't have the brain power to articulate them, coupled with massive sleep deprivation, hormones, and a general sense of having no idea what we were doing.

   We had a running joke that my husband was "Master Changer" and I was "Master Dresser" of our little guy, but that didn't mean I avoided diapers. Being the sole source of food those first few months (especially with a baby who wouldn't take a bottle) was hard, hard, hard, too. It was easy to feel like I was giving more than my fair share. In reality, though, we were both trying our best and were utterly exhausted. It wasn't until we started making monthly date nights a priority that I remembered the "us" that was there before we became three and really focused on how committed we both were to being equal partners in this parenting adventure. Now, five years later, we are still negotiating who is doing what for whom and when on a daily basis.

2. **Parents and in-laws.** Oh, where to begin?! They raised children in a different time, right? A time when so much was so different . . . and even things that were probably the same are likely foggy in their memories. My in-laws

were incredibly quick to offer advice when our first was born, and things went downhill quickly over something silly like swaddling our baby. Our son was four months old, we were "still" swaddling him, and if we didn't quit soon, he would be addicted to it and walking down the aisle of his wedding in a swaddle. I am incredibly grateful that my husband was willing to be honest with his parents and set a boundary: no advice unless requested. And, they have more or less agreed. They are incredibly loving and supportive grandparents, and having some boundaries makes for enjoyable visits all around.

3. **Think about you, mama.** Here you are, surrounded by a village of human beings, small and large, probably every single moment of every single day. A miracle, honor, wonder, and blessing? Yes. And potentially overwhelming. If you are an introvert like I am, the complete and utter lack of personal or alone time in your day can come as a bit of a shock. Going from work to parenting to partner time to crashing into slumber to be awakened by a baby is something brand new to navigate, and you may not even realize how much it is affecting you. I, for one, am certainly more irritable around the important members of my village if I don't get my alone time—even a few minutes of it—every day. This is just something to take stock of and plan for.

With all this in mind, I offer you a few tips to help you maintain sanity within that village of yours:

- **Assume positive intent.** This goes a long way with partners, parents, in-laws, colleagues—you name it.

- **Don't stew.** If something is bothering you, do not let it fester. Problems always seem to become larger when they're not addressed?

- **Go with your gut.** You may be a new parent, but you are the person who knows your child the best. If your parents are insisting on evening activities and you feel like your baby is on the verge of a meltdown, listen to that instinct and do what you need to do.

- **Draw boundaries that keep you sane.** For me and my husband, one of the biggest boundaries we drew was to start staying at a hotel rather than at my in-law's house when we went to visit. This was not met with huge amounts of enthusiasm, as you can imagine, but it serves to maintain truly positive relationships.

- **Let go when you can.** If your partner has the baby and you are off somewhere else in the house doing something else, *let go* of that need to intervene and step in. Everyone has different ways to soothe a child, and the more practice he or she gets, the better for everyone.

- **Work that gratitude practice.** Go back to our lesson from Chapter 2 and remember to "find the good." Some member of that village may be driving you absolutely crazy right now, but is there something about their presence you can be grateful for?

Be kind to yourself as you think about these relationships, mama. A whole new world is unfolding right now, and you *will* find a place in it that feels right for you.

CAPITALIZATION:
SHARE THE JOY WITH YOUR COMMUNITY

"Good, the more communicated, more abundant grows."
— John Milton, *Paradise Lost: Book V*

Today as you build and maintain your communities, I encourage you to start thinking about what you take the time to share and with whom. There is a concept called "capitalization" that a clinical psychiatrist friend of mine introduced me to, one that I absolutely love. In the theory of capitalization, "communicating personal positive events with others [is] associated with increased positive affect and well-being, above and beyond the impact of the positive event itself and other daily events." In other words, if something good happens to you, everybody gets more benefit from that something good if you actually *talk about it.*

Since learning about this idea, I have been working harder at the end of each day to think back to a success I had at work or with the kids and sharing it with my husband. Not only does taking the time to think back through positive things that happened during the day help me focus on the good and savor it, but pushing myself to share these things has been good for our relationship, too. I hear my win or victory reflected back in a kind and compassionate way, and my husband learns more about my day.

Spreading the joy of positive events requires thinking about those with whom you can share your good news and with whom you can't. I definitely have friends who will jump up and down with me when I have even the smallest success to share. On the other hand, there are other people in my life who will downplay my news or be jealous of any successes.

You don't need big wins or major life events to happen to reap the benefits of capitalization. Any small, happy event or success—from getting your baby to fall asleep to finishing up a memo you've been writing—will work. The literature shows that the more people you tell, the more magnified the effects. So don't hold back—share and multiply all that good with those in your community who will reflect all that goodness back to you.

Chapter 6

CONCLUSION

Congratulations, mama. If you made it to this chapter in the book, you are completely committed to success as a working parent, and you are going to be *just fine*. (And, I'll note, you were going to be just fine, even if you didn't make it to this chapter.) Through these pages, you've come a long way in exploring your return to work. You've stretched your muscles around gratitude and perspective, mapped out some returning-to-work logistics, reflected on leadership opportunities, and thought about what communities you need in your life. It has been an honor to be one of your (hopefully many!) guides on this new working mother journey, and I hope you found this book both fun and helpful.

I would love to hear from you in your journey. Send any questions you have about how to navigate this return-from-maternity-leave thing or life as a working parent to me at lori@mindfulreturn.com, and I promise to respond both with an answer and a discount to the Mindful Return E-Course. I would love to have you as part of this amazing community of strong and brilliant mamas.

I leave you now with two final sections for fun and inspiration. From the first, I wish you a laugh; from the second, I hope you feel the hug coming through the pages of this book.

THE LETTER I REALLY WANTED TO SEND MY EMPLOYER

Dear Employer,

I'm about to come back from maternity leave and there are a few things I want to make sure you know before you see me.

First and foremost, I am looking forward with *great* excitement to having intellectually stimulating conversations with you in a clean, quiet office.

Now to confirm and deny a few things you may be thinking:

Yes, it *is* true that I won't be the same person I was before I left, and also that I may not be completely and entirely "with it" for the first few months. No one whose sleep has been interrupted every two hours for weeks on end or whose body was just turned upside down and inside out possibly could be.

Yes, it *is* true that I may never look like the gunners down the hall who stay at the office until 8:00 pm every night and never take a sick day or vacation day. My day care does close at 5:45 pm sharp, I do get charged $10 per minute if I'm late, and that little petri dish of a baby will get some awful bugs. But you can count of me to be back online after bedtime. . . and I won't miss a deadline.

Yes, it *is* true I love my baby. And my career. I am not conflicted about loving both. But I do feel pulled in many directions every day.

No, it is *not* true that I have somehow lost value to you. No, I don't waste hours of my day pumping milk. Did you know I've learned to hold the pump with one hand and type with the other? And while you may not see it yet through the bleary eyes or ponytail, I am and will be a leader in your organization. I anticipate the needs of others—clients and screaming babies—in ways you have never imagined. I prioritize like nobody's business. I am more efficient than anyone on the team. I also have a newfound superpower of connecting with people—colleagues, clients, you name it—thanks to this fundamental thing many people do called *having children.*

I have a few small requests for when I come back. Meet these, and you will win my unending loyalty. Cut me some slack the first few months. I won't be sleep-deprived forever (or so the experienced parents tell me), but for the moment I am. Be kind. Ask about my child. When my kids get sick, tell me to take care of them first, and mean it. Don't expect me to return unchanged by motherhood; but do expect me to be an amazing, talented, intelligent, and thoughtful employee. Keep me around and engaged in the work that's going on. You won't regret it.

See you soon,
Mindfully Returning Mama

THE BEST ANTIDOTE TO GUILT I KNOW

To close, I am sharing with you with a letter I wrote myself when I struggled with a lot of the topics I wrote about in this book. It was truly a loving voice of reason speaking to me, and I hope you hear her call, too.

Dearest Lori:

You are enough.

You got this, mama. This thing called parenthood. This thing called life. Called friendship. Called career woman. You don't have to please everyone to be enough. Heck, you don't need to please ANYONE to be enough. You just ARE.

What you've accomplished today is already enough. What you've accomplished this week is already enough. What you've done in your career is already enough. What you've been able to do in this one wild and crazy life is already enough. Enough doing. Enough accomplishing. Enough checks off the to-do list. It's time to BE enough. Because you already ARE.

Don't change a thing, and you are enough. Sufficient. Complete. Perfect. Beautiful. Ever-growing, ever-changing, yes, but enough at each phase. Each stage. Each breath. Each hug. Each love.

Sometimes you may see disorder and chaos, never-ending to-do lists. Dishes that refill the sink ad nauseam. But even through all that, you have done enough. You WILL keep moving, growing, living, mothering, cleaning, working, playing . . . whether or not you worry about it, plan it all out, or belittle yourself about it. You WILL keep on keeping on. While being enough. TRULY.

Trust yourself. Your intuition. Your sense of smell. Your sense of politics. Your heart. Your good intentions. Your growth. Your family. Love it all, and trust that YOU GOT THIS.

You are a pretty awesome mother, woman, grower, lover, friend, wife, neighbor, and colleague, my dear, sweet mama. You deserve to believe this about yourself. And to know, in your heart of hearts, that you don't need to be fixed, perfected, corrected, brought down a peg, or taught a few things. You are ALREADY enough. Whether you write in a journal or not. Do that reading assignment or not. Cry today or not. Laugh today or not. Whatever happens today. Or tomorrow. Or the next day. You got it. You will KEEP getting it. I love you, my dear, sweet young mama. You are enough.

To all my dear mamas reading this book: can you see yourselves as enough today?

AFTERWARD

KEEP IN TOUCH WITH MINDFUL RETURN

Thank you, mama, for joining me on this journey to help the leave-and-return experience go more smoothly. I would love to keep in touch with you! Here's how:

- Email me anytime at lori@mindfulreturn.com.

- Sign up for my weekly newsletter, Saturday Secrets, by going to www.mindfulreturn.com.

- Will you be heading out on maternity leave or heading back to work soon? Join an online community of mamas who are all doing this at the same time as you—and work the principles of this book through journal prompts and group discussions—by joining a session of the Mindful Return Course. Go to www.mindfulreturn.com/e-course to sign up. After you take the course, you will have lifetime access to the private Mindful Return alumnae community on Facebook. This alumnae community is an amazing group of working mamas active in supporting one another in this working motherhood journey.

- "Like" the Mindful Return page on Facebook at www.facebook.com/mindfulreturn.

- Follow Mindful Return on Twitter! @mindfulreturn

BACK TO WORK AFTER BABY

RESOURCES

We are lucky to live in an age where resources for new working mamas are abundant—and growing by the minute! Please see www.mindfulreturn.com/resources for a comprehensive list of reading suggestions and additional supports. For starters, here are six of my favorite books for working moms:

OVERWHELMED

WORK, LOVE, AND PLAY WHEN NO ONE HAS THE TIME, by Brigid Schulte

- **Why read it?** It's the current BIBLE for understanding the life of working parents. It's as fascinating as it is readable.

- **Favorite quote?** It's hard to choose given I've dog-eared about 50 pages—here, Brigid is quoting Eugene O'Kelly, former CEO, KPMG. "What if I hadn't worked so hard? What if . . . I had actually used . . . my position to be a role model for balance? Had I done so intentionally, who's to say that, besides having more time with my family, I wouldn't also have been even more focused at work? More creative? More productive? It took inoperable late stage brain cancer to get me to examine things from this angle."

HERE'S THE PLAN

YOUR PRACTICAL, TACTICAL GUIDE TO
ADVANCING YOUR CAREER DURING
PREGNANCY AND PARENTING, by Allyson Downey

- **Why read it?** You're pregnant or a new working parent, and you're learning the logistical ropes of planning for maternity leave, returning, and finding family-friendly workplaces. I love her checklists related to things like "Questions to ask HR" before you go on maternity leave, and the straight up pros and cons of the various child care options.

- **Favorite quote?** " . . . [E]very day that you put yourself out there as the rock star you are, you're poking a hole in someone's unconscious bias against mothers. They might not be aware of it—you might not be aware of it—but you're registering as someone who delivers, no matter the circumstances . . . .When you share an idea that's a game changer or finish a project that's challenged all of your colleagues, you're offering proof positive that whether or not you have a child isn't part of the equation that calculates professional success."

DARING GREATLY

HOW THE COURAGE TO BE VULNERABLE
TRANSFORMS THE WAY WE LIVE, LOVE,
PARENT, AND LEAD, by Brené Brown

- **Why read it?** Because we can all learn a thing or two about vulnerability, and we are all daring greatly at this parenthood thing. Her title quotes Teddy Roosevelt's speech: "It is not the critic who counts; not the man who points out how the strong man stumbles . . . The credit belongs to the man who is actually in the area, whose face is marred by dust and sweat and blood; who strives valiantly; who errs, who comes short again and again . . . and who at the worst, if he fails, at least fails while daring greatly."

- **Favorite quote?** Her "Wholehearted Parenting Manifesto" (see pages 244-45), the last line of which reads, "I will not teach or love or show you anything perfectly, but I will let you see me, and I will always hold sacred the gift of seeing you. Truly, deeply, seeing you."

NURTURING THE SOUL OF YOUR FAMILY

10 WAYS TO RECONNECT AND FIND PEACE IN EVERYDAY LIFE, by Renée Peterson Trudeau

- **Why read it?** I read this book while nursing my youngest (and, truth be told, while holding him for various weekend naps), and just the act of reading it calmed me down. Trudeau is great at helping you assess what's working and not in your own family life, giving great journaling prompts, and encouraging baby steps toward change.

- **Favorite quote?** "Our kids' behavior is inextricably tried to our emotional well-being. If things around us are in disequilibrium or are out of sync, we need to have the courage to examine if we're in disequilibrium. What's going on with our inner world, our lens, and how we're viewing life in general? Often this becomes a wake-up call to begin to parent more consciously and to explore if a course correction is needed on our part."

MITTEN STRINGS FOR GOD

REFLECTIONS FOR MOTHERS IN A HURRY,
by Katrina Kenison

- **Why read it?** It's beautiful bedtime reading. Each chapter is an exquisitely written essay, perfect for soaking in one at a time before bed each night. Kenison helped me as a new mama to calm down, zoom out, and view the beauty of motherhood from a new perspective.

- **Favorite quote?** "One of my greatest challenges each day is to sustain an atmosphere in our home that nourishes not only our bodies and intellects, but our inner lives as well. To do so, I need to have some kind of vision of where the ideal really lies. I need a sense of balance. So I ask myself, How do I want to be in the world? How shall my children spend their days? How will I spend my own? I've learned that when I'm uncertain myself of what we really need or want, I tend to charge ahead, swept up in the busyness of life. But when I take the time to examine our choices—when I make decisions thoughtfully and from the heart, I almost always end up paring down and cutting back, doing less and enjoying it more."

DELIGHT

EIGHT PRINCIPLES FOR LIVING WITH JOY AND EASE, by Pleasance Silicki

- **Why read it?** This short e-book helps you step back from "crazy busy" to think about how you might live in a different way. I loved Silicki's personal stories, practical self-care exercises, and straightforward thoughts on how to live a more mindful life.

- **Favorite quote?** "When people ask you, 'How are you?'— instead of the same old, 'Crazy busy' answer, try saying, 'Good. I live with joy and ease.' If you don't see your life that way quite yet, don't worry. You will. Open your mind and heart and think the mantra, 'It's possible.' "